MW01114764

To Linda,

Color Me a Woman of God: Break Me, Melt Me, Mold Me, Fill Me and Use Me

God's story is your story! Jer. 29:11

Cheryl

Color Me A Woman of God:

Break Me, Melt Me, Mold Me, Fill Me and Use Me

How to be Fruitful and Fulfilled in Christ
in an Unequally Yoked Relationship

Cheryl Torain

Copyright © 2008 by Cheryl Torain

All rights reserved. No part of this book may be reproduced in any form without permission from the publisher, except in the case of brief quotations embodied in critical articles or reviews.

All Scripture quotations in this publication are taken from the MacArthur Study Bible – New King James Version Copyright 1997

Cover Design: Patricia Payne
Photographer: Stephanie Hopkins

ISBN: 978-0-615-19048-8

Printed in the United States of America

Contents

This book is dedicated
to my Lord and Savior Jesus Christ
Who predestined, called, justified
and one day will glorify me.

I also dedicate this book to my daughters
Zena and Tasha
who have been my pillars of love
and encouragement throughout this journey.

Acknowledgements

Parents - James and Blanche Williams

Siblings - Brenda, Ronald, Larry and Kathy

Pastor of Genesis Bible Fellowship Ministries
    - Pastor Wayne Cockrell

Prayer Warriors - Glenda Spence and Deborah Meadows

Armor Bearers - Brenda Briscoe, Darlene Ford, Glenda
Spence, Jackie Cheeks, Faith Williams, Lee Doris Palmer and
Linda Johnson

Harrison Hill and Ricky Felder - Musicians

My extended family, Genesis Bible Fellowship Ministries,
and co-laborers in the Gospel who have touched my life these
35 years.

       Thank you!   Thank you!   Thank you!

Introduction

COLOR fills our world with beauty. We delight in the colors of a magnificent sunset and in the bright red and golden - yellow of autumn. We are charmed by gorgeous flowering plants and the brilliantly colored arch of a rainbow. We also use color in various ways to add pleasure and interest to our lives.

Color serves as a means of communication. In sports, players have different colored uniforms to display their particular team. On streets and highways, a red traffic light tells drivers to stop, and a green light tells them to go.

We use the name of colors to describe moods and feelings. For example, we say a sad person *feels blue* and a jealous one is *green with envy*. We say an angry person *sees red*. A coward may be called *yellow*. (**World Book Encyclopedia**)

God has created all things for His glory. **Colossians 1:16 "For by Him all things were created that are in heaven and that are on earth, visible and invisible, whether thrones or dominions or principalities or powers. All things were created through Him and for Him."** Our lives, as creatures of a sovereign God, are colored throughout this journey called life. We share a kaleidoscope of good times and bad times, sunny days and cloudy days. But for the Christian, we should see our journey as a kaleidoscope of trials and blessings. So will you journey with me and dare to say:

Color Me a Woman of God: Break Me, Melt Me, Mold Me, Fill Me and Use Me?

Color Me A Woman of God:
Break Me
(Jesus Specializes in Brokenness)

J EREMIAH 18:1-6 says "The word which came to Jeremiah from the LORD, saying: "Arise and go down to the potter's house, and there I will cause you to hear My words." Then I went down to the potter's house, and there he was, making something at the wheel. And the vessel that he made of clay was marred in the hand of the potter; so he made it again into another vessel, as it seemed good to the potter to make. Then the word of the LORD came to me, saying: "O house of Israel, can I not do with you as this potter?" says the LORD. "Look, as the clay *is* in the potter's hand, so *are* you in My hand, O house of Israel!"

The year is 1965. I am 18 years old and fresh out of high school with a new job and a new man, Raymond. Oh how exciting is young love! But, then the unexpected happened. I found out that I was pregnant. So doing the right thing at 19 years old, I got married. I then had two miscarriages in the first five years of marriage.

> *Life can only be understood by looking backward,*
> *but it must be lived by looking forward.*

Life doesn't stop with your pain, it goes on. There comes a point in this journey of life when your heart asks the question: "Why am I here and what is my purpose in life?" By 1970, I had a beautiful daughter Zena and a nice home, but my marriage had begun to go through a time of dryness. You see, God will create a desert and emptiness in your life that will cause you to begin to thirst for Him. I knew something was missing, but I did not know what.

By September 1972, my sister, Brenda (she will always say that I am her older sister) had changed. This one who loved to party had a new conversation. Brenda shared with me how she had come to know Jesus Christ as her personal Savior. She, in turn, had been challenged by a homosexual Jew who had been converted by the power of the Gospel. Truly, our God is awesome! This encounter would ultimately lead my entire family (now 22 and still counting) in coming to the saving knowledge of Jesus Christ, all but my brother Ronald and husband Raymond.

In October 1972, while attending a revival service at Manna Bible Baptist Church in Baltimore, Maryland, I accepted Jesus Christ as my personal Savior. Also, at this time my beautiful daughter Tasha was born. Little did I know that my life and my marriage would never be the same. **"For I know the thoughts that I think towards you, says the Lord, thoughts of peace and not of evil, to give you a future and hope. Then you will call upon Me and go and pray to Me, and I will listen to you. And you will seek Me and find Me, when you search for Me with all your heart."** (Jeremiah 29:11)

I was born again! My heart had changed! A new passion, joy and peace had invaded my soul. My sins had been forgiven and I now looked at life through new spiritual lens. I had to go home and share this good news with my husband, but I had a rude awakening. **"Can two walk together except they agree?"** (Amos 3:3) There was no agreement as to this new love relationship that I had found. Luke 14:26 says "If anyone comes to Me and does not hate (love less) his father and mother, wife (or husband) and children, brothers and sisters, yes, and his own life also, he cannot be My disciple."

> *Conversion is the miracle of a moment; becoming like*
> *Christ is the work of a lifetime.*
>
> *(Our Daily Bread)*

At the royal palace of Tehran in Iran (which was previously Persia) you see one of the most beautiful mosaic works in the world. The ceilings and walls flash like diamonds and multi-faceted reflections. Originally when the palace was designed, the architect specified that he wanted huge sheets of mirrors on the walls. When the first shipment arrived from Paris, he found that the mirrors were shattered. The contractor threw them in the trash and brought the sad news to the architect. But the architect ordered that all of the broken pieces be collected. He smashed them into tiny pieces and glued them to the walls to become a mosaic of silvery, shimmery, mirrored pieces of glass.

Broken dreams, broken marriages, broken lives... As God directed Jeremiah down to the potter's house to watch clay being molded, God was announcing that the potter and the clay illustrated His relationship to His people Israel. They were like clay in His hands. God has a right to tear down or build up a nation. He promised the nation blessing; but since Israel continued to do evil, He would reconsider the good He intended and bring judgment. If Israel would turn from her evil ways, God would revoke the disaster.

God has to transform our false precepts of life. For example, we aren't satisfied with being a homemaker. One day we look up and see women with three-piece suits and prestigious positions and it seems as if they have it all together. Being the average homemaker, we become discontent. Being discontent, we then have to find ourselves. Many working women have realized that they settled for God's permissive will instead of His perfect will. **"And He gave them their request, but sent leanness into their soul." (Psalm 106:15)** Their jobs didn't fulfill them as they thought it would and they didn't really find themselves. If anything, their lives became much more complicated. Even as married women, we look to marriage as an avenue of meeting our needs. We have these great expectations, but we find that those expectations are unrealistic, so we become frustrated and dissatisfied and women of broken dreams.

There is a poem that says: "As children bring broken toys with tears for us to mend, I brought my broken dreams to God because He was my friend. But then instead of leaving Him in peace to work alone, I hung around and tried to help with ways that were my own. At last I snatched them back and cried, Lord, how can you be so slow? My child, He said, what could I do, you never let them go." You and I are women with broken dreams, broken marriages and broken lives **until we meet Jesus.**

> *It is impossible for the woman to despair who remembers that her Helper is omnipotent.*

As Israel looked around, they wanted change, but they became hardheaded and stubborn. God used Jeremiah, directing him as the weeping prophet, to go to His people to compel them to become obedient to the Word of God. The people responded by saying that they were helpless to change. They said it was useless. They stubbornly continued to follow the plans of their hearts. The nation turned to idolatry. They turned away from the Lord.

The Japanese have an ingenious way of changing the color and appearance of birds and animals. For example, white sparrows are produced by selecting a pair of grayish birds and keeping them in a white cage, in a white room where they are attended by a person dressed in white. The mental effect on a series of generations of birds results in completely white birds. God, too, has an ingenious way of changing sinners into saints and He specializes in **BROKENNESS!**

The heart is desperately wicked, and no one can know it except God. **"The heart is deceitful above all things, and desperately wicked; who can know it? I, the LORD, search the heart; I test the mind, even to give every man according to his ways, according to the fruit of his doings."** (Jeremiah 17:9) The Scripture says that all of our righteousness is as filthy rags. Those filthy rags are like the rags of a woman on her menstrual cycle. There are no works of righteousness that we can perform to merit salvation, but to accept it as a gift. Ephesians 2:8-9 **"For by grace you have been saved through faith, and not of yourselves; it is the gift of God, not of works, lest anyone should boast."** God has to break us before He can even begin to **melt, mold, fill and use us.**

> *There is no pit so deep that Jesus is not deeper still.*
> *(Corrie Ten Boom)*

Finding Fulfillment

Question: Have you accepted Jesus Christ as your personal Savior? If you are not sure, make your calling and election sure.

Challenge: Pray this prayer: "Lord Jesus, I know that I am a sinner and deserve to pay the penalty for my sins. I believe that Jesus Christ died for my sins on the cross of Calvary and rose from the dead. I accept Him into my heart and life as my personal Savior."

> Romans 10:13 "For whoever calls on the name of the Lord shall be saved."

There are six evidences of salvation according to the Bible:

(1) You will have a new love for Scripture. **I Peter 2:2 "As newborn babes desire the pure milk of the Word that you may grow thereby."**

(2) You will have an awareness of right and wrong. **Hebrews 5:13-14 says "For everyone who partakes only of milk is unskilled in the word of righteousness, for he is a babe. But solid food belongs to those who are of full age, that is, those who by reason of use have their senses exercised to discern both good and evil."**

(3) You will have a desire to be like Jesus. **Romans 8:29 says "For whom He foreknew, He also predestined to be conformed to the image of His Son, that He might be the firstborn among many brethren."**

(4) There will be pressure from people you once associated with. **I Peter 4:3-4 says "For we have spent enough of our past lifetime in doing the will of the Gentiles—when we walked in lewdness, lusts, drunkenness, revelries, drinking parties, and abominable idolatries. In regard to these, they think**

it strange that you do not run with them in the same flood of dissipation, speaking evil of you."

(5) You will have a desire to proclaim Christ to others. Colossians 1:28-29 says "Him we preach, warning every man and teaching every man in all wisdom, that we may present every man perfect in Christ Jesus. To this end I also labor, striving according to His working which works in me mightily."

(6) You will have a love for Christians. I John 3:14 says "We know that we have passed from death to life, because we love the brethren. He who does not love his brother abides in death."

Brokenness not only leads to salvation, but as the Potter begins the educational process of conforming us into women of God, there must be "divine discipline." I was now in training. Hebrews 12:11 says "Now no chastening seems to be joyful for the present, but painful; nevertheless, afterward it yields a peaceable fruit of righteousness to those who have been trained by it." Divine discipline is an evidence of God's divine love. Oh what love the Lord was showing me.

> *In order to receive the direction from God, you must be able to receive the correction from God.*

The breaking process involves divine discipline as an evidence of divine love because:

a. It is part of the educational process by which a believer is fitted to share God's holiness.

b. It is poof of a genuine love relationship between the heavenly
    Father and His children.
c. It helps train us to be obedient.
d. It produces character.

God has given four structures of authority: family, government,
church and business. He conforms us into the image of His Son by
putting us under one or more of these umbrellas of authority.

When the Lord chastens us, it is to prove that He loves us and
that we are in a relationship with Him. The Lord wants to protect
us. Sometimes we forget that outside of the umbrella of protection
is the enemy. "**Be sober; be vigilant, because your adversary the
devil walks about like a roaring lion, seeking whom he may
devour. Resist him, steadfast in the faith, knowing that the same
sufferings are experienced by your brotherhood in the world.**" (I
Peter 5:8-9)

The word for "devil" means "slanderer," thus a malicious
enemy who maligns believers. He and his forces are always
active, looking for opportunities to overwhelm the believer
with temptation, persecution, and discouragement. Satan sows
discord, accuses God to men, men to God, and men to men. (**The
MacArthur Study Bible**) He cannot take our salvation, but he
desires to unravel our fellowship with Christ and take us out of
Christian service.

"Resist" means "to stand up against." The way to resist him is
by remaining firm in the Christian faith. I had to "resist" a rebellious
spirit, an unsubmissive spirit and an unloving spirit. Sometimes
I was victorious and sometimes I lost the battle. We always have
the tendency to feel as though "we are the only one going through
this situation." However, the Lord was again teaching me that my
marriage was my umbrella of protection - with holes.

If you are in a para-ministry, your pastor is your umbrella of protection. Parents are their children's umbrella of protection. There will always be injustice on our jobs, but we must learn to be under the umbrella of authority of our supervisors. God knows how to provide an open door of escape when necessary and He says, "Vengeance is Mine."

> *The ultimate measure of a man (or woman) is not where they stand in moments of comfort and convenience, but where they stand at times of challenge and controversy.*
>
> *(Martin Luther King)*

Daniel responded right to authority, thereby, having God's favor upon his life. When we do things according to our own desires and will, we make trouble for ourselves. Therefore, we should maintain close fellowship with the Lord and ask for wisdom in our circumstances. As the Lord, in His humanity was obedient to God the Father, how much more should we be obedient to the Lord because of His great forgiveness.

Hebrews 12:9 says **"Furthermore, we have had human fathers who corrected *us*, and we paid *them* respect. Shall we not much more readily be in subjection to the Father of spirits and live?"** When our parents chastened us, it helped us to grow. It did not always feel good, but when done in wisdom we learned some things. Respect for God equals submission to His will, and those who willingly receive the Lord's chastening will have a richer, more abundant life.

Chastisement must be accepted with the right spirit for the right result. It is not a matter of accepting a minor chastisement with grace, but seeing chastisement as a "habit of life." When that's present, then "the peaceable fruit of righteousness follows."

Abraham had a life of highs and lows. As Abraham had more

and more victory in his faith walk, God ultimately tested Abraham by having him offer up his son Isaac, the son of promise (**Genesis 22:1-19**). Abraham's test was not a temptation, but was God's way of showing Abraham what was in his heart. As Abraham came to Mt. Moriah, he had to leave his servants to go to that place of sacrifice to worship God. **Brokenness** is a place of sacrifice and worship that you go alone when God speaks to your heart. When Abraham obeyed by offering Isaac on the altar, not only did his faith mature, but he went to another place in his worship. He experienced a new name for God "**The-LORD-Will-Provide.**"

Our answer to prayers is in our obedience. The answer is sometimes "behind us" after we obey as "the ram was already caught in the thicket behind Abraham." Having passed the test, God proved His genuine love by providing a ram for the sacrifice instead of Abraham's son, and the peaceable fruit of righteousness flourished in Abraham's heart in a climate of spiritual peace.

> *Success seems to be connected with action.*
> *Successful people keep moving. They make mistakes,*
> *but they don't quit.*

Finding Fulfillment

Question: Who or what is your Isaac that God is testing you?

Challenge: Place that person or thing on God's altar. Choose to worship God and give thanks for His answer.

Raymond did not want Jesus as his personal Savior, yet, he saw me as a different woman. The Lord was "**breaking me.**" He said that I was not the same. Yes, I was different because II **Corinthians 5:17 says "Therefore, if anyone is in Christ, he is a**

new creation, old things have passed away; behold, all things
have become new."

After a person is regenerated, old value systems, priorities,
beliefs, loves, and plans are seen differently. Evil and sin are still
present, but the believer sees them in a new perspective, and they
no longer control him. This new walk would be a continuous
process. As the saying goes: "I became a work in progress!" My
heart ached for my husband's salvation, but God answered my
prayers by saving Zena at the age of five and Tasha at the age of
four.

> *Each relationship nurtures a strength or weakness
> within you.*

Thus began the process of God conforming me into the image
of Jesus Christ. I would be broken, melted, molded, filled and
then able to be used for His glory. My marriage would be the
instrument God would use for this process. "Being confident of
this very thing, He who has begun a good work in you shall
complete it until the day of Jesus Christ." (Philippians 1:6) My
journey for 32 years as a believer married to an unbeliever would
teach me a depth of love and fulfillment that could only be found
in Jesus Christ and Him alone.

> *Pain is inevitable, but misery is optional.*
> *(Barbara Johnson)*

Marriage is a covenant between three people: man, woman
and God. It is not to be entered into lightly, because God holds
us accountable for the vows we make. It matters not whether
you were unsaved before you got married or not, you still made
a vow before God. "When you make a vow to God, do not delay

to pay it; for He has no pleasure in fools. Pay what you have vowed - better not to vow than to vow and not pay." (Ecclesiastes 5:4-5) When a believer presumes upon the Lord and marries an unbeliever, they are going against II Corinthians 6:14 "Do not be unequally yoked together with unbelievers. For what fellowship has righteousness with lawlessness? And what communion has light with darkness?" Light and darkness can never mix. Oh, you think he will change once you marry him, but then you wake up and realize that you are now sleeping with the enemy.

> *Not everything that is faced can be changed,*
> *but nothing can be changed until it is faced.*
> *(James Baldwin)*

The Word of God says in I Corinthians 7:14-15 "For the unbelieving husband is sanctified by the wife, and the unbelieving wife is sanctified by the husband; otherwise your children would be unclean, but now they are holy. But if the unbeliever departs, let him depart; a brother or a sister is not under bondage in such cases. But God has called us to peace." Well, I had my own agenda of what would give me peace.

Did I ever want to leave? Of course! Did he ever want to leave? Of course! But he chose not to leave and God provided me with no scriptural grounds. So I prayed and asked God for His direction and wisdom. James 1:5 "If any of you lacks wisdom, let him ask of God, who gives to all liberally and without reproach, and it will be given to him." Only divine wisdom enables believers to be joyous and submissive in the trials of life.

> *The best way out of a difficulty is through it.*

As I began to thirst for the Word of God, I began to grow spiritually. I was faithful in my commitment to the things of the Lord, but it was too much for my husband. He insisted that I only attend church on Sunday mornings. Upset, yes, but the Holy Spirit was teaching me a new way of responding. **Hebrews 6:10 "Christ learned obedience by the things He suffered."** I submitted never realizing God's ultimate plan.

> *Never change God's facts into hopes or prayers,*
> *but simply accept them as you believe them.*
> *(H.W. Webb Peploe)*

For one year I was a SMO Christian, a Sunday Morning Only Christian. The Holy Spirit showed me that my growth was not only dependent upon how I participated in church, but much more on my intimacy with Christ on a daily basis. Therefore, my thirst for the Word led me to purchase a Bible commentary, dictionary and other study tools. After one year, the Lord dealt with my husband's heart and I returned to church functioning in other ministries on a consistent basis. What the enemy meant for evil, God meant for good.

Proverbs 21:1 "The king's heart is in the hand of the Lord. Like the rivers of water; He turns it wherever He wishes." That test prepared me to be what I am today: a Women's Bible Teacher.

Finding Fulfillment

Question: What is your specific area of testing at this time?

Challenge: Ask the Holy Spirit to give you a thirst for the Word of God so that "truth" and not feelings will guide you.

> *Marriage is the only union that can't be organized*
> *because both sides think they're management.*
>   *(Funny Funny World)*

Marriage provides us with an umbrella of protection, but, remember, some umbrellas have holes. The Bible states that even if our mate is not saved, or if he is carnal, you and I are still to submit **as unto the Lord.** We are instructed in **I Peter 3:1 "Wives, likewise, be submissive to your own husband, that even if some do not obey the word, they without a word, may be won by the conduct of their wives…"**

Some women married to a Christian man can also be spiritually unequally yoked. You love and serve the Lord, but he has no desire and no commitment to the things of Christ. The world says, "Leave, the grass is greener on the other side. You should be happy." But, God's principles do not change because of our circumstances. I know that some of you have turned me off and your attitude has gone into reverse because of the principle of submission, but please hear me out. If the grass looks greener on the other side of the fence, **you can bet the water bill is higher!**

God has given the authority of headship to the man as the order of creation. It has nothing to do with his performance, but his position. Submit in the Greek is the word "hupotasso" which means to functionally line up. We are not inferior or second-class citizens, but have been given a position of influence by God so that marriage could have harmony. The motivation for us in submission is **Colossians 3:18 "Wives, submit to your own husbands, as is fitting in the Lord."** This means that there should be reverence for Christ that recognizes who has asked this of us and that He will hold us accountable for our actions.

> *There is nothing nobler or more admirable than when*
> *two people who see eye to eye keep house as man and*
> *wife confounding their enemies and delighting their*
> *friends.*
>
> *(Homer)*

From the beginning of my walk with Christ, submission was a foreign concept. My love for Jesus and my desire to please Him provoked me to ask Him for help! I could not do this in the flesh, but only by the supernatural power of the Holy Spirit. Yet, this road of submission would be God's way of instructing and maturing me in the knowledge of His will for my life. I John 2:29 says **"If you know that He is righteous you know that everyone who practices righteousness is born of Him."** My obligation was to do the right thing. The rest was in God's hands.

Finding Fulfillment

Question: What authority in your life are you being challenged to submit to? Your mate? Your employer? Your Pastor?

Challenge: Ask the Lord to give you a heart to see submission from a Biblical perspective.

A. W. Tozier said "I doubt that God can use a man (or a woman) greatly until He has hurt them deeply. Standfast! God's hand is in your heartache. If you weren't important, do you think He would take this long and work this hard on your life? Those whom God uses most effectively have been hammered, filed and tempered in the furnace of trials and heartache." (**Chuck Swindoll, "Encourage Me"**) Being hammered and tempered was not my idea of growth, but my insufficient faith needed to mature and God's purposes for my life were being fulfilled.

The days turned into months, the months into years and I wondered why Raymond had not come to the Lord. You see, I was faithful to the Lord and I felt that He "owed" me his salvation by now because it had been 16 years. I got angry with the Lord because many of my friends' husbands were coming to Christ, but not mine. I had to be real with the Lord with what was in my heart because He already knew and He could handle my emotions. God used Pastor Wayne Cockrell to challenge me with the fact that God was still in control and His time would be the right time. My responsibility was to continue to be faithful.

> *I am more and more convinced that our happiness or unhappiness depends far more on the way we meet the events of life than on the nature of those events themselves.*
>
> *(Wilhelm Von Humbolt)*

Proverbs 4:23 says "Keep your heart with all diligence for out of it springs the issues of life." I cried out to the Lord so many times to keep my heart from growing bitter. In turn, the Holy Spirit was showing me how sinful my heart was and my marriage was being used to smooth out the rough edges.

Many times we are looking at what our mate is doing or not doing, and yet we have a beam in our own eyes. The Bible says in Matthew 7:3-5 "And why do you look at the speck in your brother's eye, but do not consider the plank in your own eye? Or how can you say to your brother, let me remove the speck from your eye; and look, a plank is in your own eye? Hypocrite! First remove the plank from your own eye, and then you will see clearly to remove the speck from your brother's eye."

> *If you are all wrapped up in yourself, you are overdressed.*
>
> *(Kate Halverson)*

I was humbled many times by my own unChristlike attitude. The Bible says "**The sacrifices of God are a broken spirit, a broken and a contrite heart, these, O God, You will not despise.**" (Psalm 51:17) I needed a heart and attitude change!

> *Jesus is a friend Who knows all your faults and still loves you anyway.*

Finding Fulfillment

Question: What is the plank in your eye that God wants you to deal with?
Challenge: Be "real" about what the Holy Spirit reveals to you. Call your sin what God calls it.

Someone has said that attitude is 90% how you take it and 10% how you make it. Some of us have attitudes, mega and mini attitudes, but still attitudes! In an unequally yoked relationship, our children can be affected by a marital relationship where there are two attitudes of life – one humanistic and one divine. Which view do you most often display? Is there enough evidence in your home to convict you of being a believer? It is easy to portray Christlikeness at church, but the "real" person is seen behind closed doors.

What is your attitude at this time in your marriage? Do you
regret:

a) having married an unsaved man and hoping he would
   change
b) not listening to wise counsel from your pastor, parents,
   friends, etc.
c) not listening to that still small voice of the Holy Spirit
d) marrying because you were lonely and now you are
   lonelier
e) marrying because you did not want to continue to fornicate
   …regrets, regrets!

> *There is little difference in people, but that little*
> *difference makes a big difference. The little difference is*
> *attitude. The big difference is whether it is positive or*
> *negative.*
>
> (W. Clement Stone)

Remember, God is sovereign. He was not taken by surprise
by the choices we would make whether saved or not. He has
"called us with a holy calling not according to our works, but
according to His own purpose and grace which was given to us
in Christ Jesus before the world began." (II Timothy 1:9) When
Christ came, He brought a whole new approach to functional
relationships between people, and the marital relationship was
one.

There is mutual submission to one another and functional
submission in marriage, employment and government. The size
of our God is greatly determined by our ability to see how He
is able to work through those in authority over us. Taking our

place under the authority of another is an inward attitude and an outward action.

In marriage, some men have to learn that you cannot demand respect for if it is to be real and meaningful, it must be earned. Your husband is given authority in position by God, even though he is not performing! Godly submission is an invitation for the husband to be the servant leader God made him to be. Jesus condemns any behavior that indulges in a lust for power and control. We are not obligated, however, to follow leadership if it conflicts with specific scriptural commands to disobey God. Even when we have to display "tough love," it must be according to the principles of the Word of God.

I thank God that even though I was unequally yoked, there was no physical abuse. Today we have testimonies of physical and verbal abuse in Christian marriages. The Bible sets the standard of a man loving his wife as Christ loved the church. He is also challenged to love her as his "own body." I haven't heard of a man yet who beat and bruised his own body, unless he had a mental condition.

The Lord has created us with tremendous value for His glory. Abuse is the misuse of what God has made and we are never to settle for that in a relationship. When we don't understand our purpose, abuse is inevitable. Some principles to follow if you are an abused spouse:

A. Admit that you are a victim of spousal abuse. Don't take responsibility for this kind of behavior.
B. Get to a place of safety. Call a local shelter.
C. Notify the authorities as soon as possible in the event of an attack.
D. Break the silence. Tell someone you trust about the abuse and don't stop talking until someone takes you seriously.

E. If you feel there is no one, tell Jesus **"Come unto Me, all you who are weary and burdened, and I will give you rest."** (Matthew 11:28) (Radio Bible Class)

When we study the Word of God, we are able to take a biblical stand and make an appeal when necessary. In appealing to authority, we must:

a. Evaluate our attitudes and motives.

 1. An independent spirit leads to disloyalty and disunity.
 2. A condemning spirit leads to self-righteousness and pride.
 3. A defiant spirit leads to insensitivity and resistance.
 4. A bitter spirit leads to hatred and rejection.

b. Clear your own conscience with God and the person in authority. **Acts 24:16 "And I exercise myself to have always a conscience void of offence toward God and toward men."** *(Conscience is God's built-in warning system. Be very happy when it hurts you. Be very worried when it doesn't.)*

c. Discuss and share peacefully your real concerns.

d. Prayerfully create alternatives: **"good timing in approach."**

e. Appeal to the authority:

 1. Explain the benefits of your insight.
 2. Explain your personal convictions without a condemning spirit.
 3. Leave the final decision to the person in authority - **they are accountable!**

f. Give God time to change their mind.
g. Remember "due time" is God's business, so wait on Him.
   (I Peter 5:10) "…after you have suffered a while, God will make you complete, establish, strengthen, and settle you." (Bill Gothard)

Oh, how this principle of making an appeal worked in my life. After working for 13 years, I knew that the Lord was calling me into another level of commitment to women's ministry. I wanted to leave my full time employment for part time work. However, I had to discuss this with Raymond. The heated discussion produced a tension headache that hindered me from going to work the next day. But God's **due time!** Around 2 p.m. that day, Raymond called me from work and told me to do whatever was on my heart. I began walking by faith and being sustained by God's goodness on a part time basis.

Finding Fulfillment

Question: Are you giving God His due time or are you trying to help Him?

Challenge: Prayerfully consider making an appeal God's way.

The Lord has given me the privilege of participating in three mission trips to Africa, India and Brazil. Only the Lord could have touched Raymond's heart to agree for me to go. But no matter whether it was a retreat, mission trip or conference, I made sure that things were taken care of at home first. It's really hard to teach others what you are not willing to do yourself.

Oh yes my sisters, submission is hard work because it is a **work** of the heart. God said in **Proverbs 23:26** "My son (or daughter), give me your heart, and let your eyes observe my ways." God can heal a broken heart, but He has to have all the pieces.

> *To handle yourself, use your head. To handle others, use your heart.*
>
> *(John Maxwell)*

Understanding submission from God's perspective can enable you to see God's will for your life. Even when the circumstances are cloudy, remember the Lord has a plan for your life and your mate is a part of His plan to conform you to the image of His Son. We can't embrace or submit to Christ without the cross and the cross implies "brokenness." Your experiential knowledge of Christ should not be a head issue, but a **heart issue**.

> *Don't be afraid of pressure. Remember that pressure is what turns a lump of coal into a diamond.*

Color Me a Woman of God: BREAK ME!!

Color Me a Woman of God:
Melt Me
(Jesus Sits as a Refiner and Purifier)

PSALM 66:10-12

"For You, O God, have tested us; You have refined us as silver is refined. You brought us into the net; You laid affliction on our backs. You have caused men to ride over our heads; we went through fire and through water; but You brought us out to rich fulfillment."

BROKEN is to become beautiful. It is possible to become better because of the brokenness. It is extremely rare to find in the great museums of the world objects of antiquity that are unbroken. Some of the most precious pieces are only fragments that remain a hollow reminder of a glorious past. Therefore, never underestimate God's power to repair and restore the broken pieces of our lives. That's where some of us are. We feel that we are broken, and that there can be no restoration, but in the melting process, God gets our attention.

After receiving Jesus Christ as Lord and Savior, the process of sanctification began. When I married, I said "for better or for worse." The good times were good, but sometimes the bad times far exceeded what I could have imagined.

> *Give your troubles to God: He will be up all night anyway.*

We try to take one day at a time, but sometimes several days attack us at once. Satan tries to confuse us. We feel like our lives are being consumed with the cares and troubles of this world. Paul referred to these ideologies as fortresses in which people are imprisoned and need to be set free and brought captive to Christ and obedient to the truth.

Many times I would say, "Will I ever have peace or enjoy any quietness of heart?" **Ephesians 2:1-3 says "And you He made alive, who were dead in trespasses and sins, in which you once walked according to the course of this world, according to the prince of the power of the air, the spirit who now works in the sons of disobedience, among whom also we all once conducted ourselves in the lusts of our flesh, fulfilling the desires of the flesh and of the mind, and were by nature children of wrath, just as the others."** Far more than anything, I was a spiritually dead person who was made alive by God. Salvation brings spiritual life to the dead. The power that raises believers out of death and makes them alive is the same power that energizes every aspect of Christian living.

Satan can not take our salvation, but he wants to make us miserable in our salvation. **I Peter 4:12-13 says "Beloved, do not think it strange concerning the fiery trial which is to try you, as though some strange thing happened to you; but rejoice to the extent that you partake of Christ's sufferings, that when His glory is revealed, you may also be glad with exceeding joy."** God will use the fires of adversity to "melt" our hearts. When the Apostle Peter wrote this epistle, it was shortly before or after the burning of Rome and at the beginning of the horrors of a 200 - year period of Christian persecution. Peter explains that four attitudes are necessary in order to be triumphant in persecution: 1) expect it; 2) rejoice in it; 3) evaluate its cause; and 4) entrust it to God. (**The MacArthur Study Bible**)

> *It is good to remember that the tea kettle, although up to its neck in hot water, continues to sing.*

It should not seem strange that troubling circumstances befall us. We are to be overjoyed, not because of the circumstances, but because God is able to keep us in the midst of the circumstances. James 1:2-3 says **"My brethren, count it all joy when you fall into various trials, knowing that the testing of your faith produces patience."** Our natural response is not to rejoice; therefore the believer must make a conscious commitment to face them with joy. Joy is from Jesus and is characteristic of the fruit of the Spirit, but happiness depends on the right happenings or the right circumstances.

The word "trials" here denotes trouble, or something that breaks the pattern of peace, comfort, joy and happiness. The trial puts us to the test with the purpose of discovering that person's nature or that thing's quality. God brings tests to prove, increase the strength and quality of one's faith and to demonstrate its validity. Since every test of faith is designed to strengthen, if we wrongly respond, that test becomes a temptation to do evil. When we patiently endure, spiritual maturity will be evidenced and our faith will have produced a deeper and greater trust in Christ. Satan tries to discourage us, but we have to remember that our trials are part of the chastening process to melt the dross - our ugly attitudes and those peculiar ways that are totally contrary to the character of Christ.

All of us live in a sphere that encompasses our entire lives, but God is outside of that sphere. Our spheres consist of our job, our family, our friends, our church, our finances and our health. All of these areas are important to us. When God begins to refine us, He uses the furnace of affliction to invade our sphere. The Lord sovereignly touches one or more of those areas. Aren't you glad that He doesn't touch everything at one time? He is a merciful God. Not many of us have been tested like Job who lost everything in his sphere but his wife, yet he came through to say in **Job 13:15** **"Though He slay me, yet will I trust Him."**

> *You should never let adversity get you down -*
> *except on your knees.*

A crisis or stressful event is when a situation has caused a potential interruption in your normal pattern of life. This situation could entail a divorce, constant marital conflicts, children on drugs, a loved one incarcerated, an unwanted pregnancy, AIDS, death in your family and the list goes on and on. It comes as a "fiery trial" allowed by God, a temptation by Satan, or a motivation by the world or our own flesh. However, our response to this part of God's melting process is important. It will either:

(a) bring opportunity for growth or self destruction
(b) cause us to get better or become bitter
(c) cause us to become a conqueror or we will be conquered by life

Emotions take the lead in the melting process. They are very real (PMS, pre menopausal, post menopausal), you know what I am referring to. It's all about what "I" **am feeling!** As women, we are more emotional than men. That is the way God made us.

If we live by our emotions, our lives will be chaotic with plenty of drama. We have to allow the Spirit of God to bring our emotions under His control.

> *If you feel "dog tired" at night, maybe it's*
> *because you "growled" all day.*

I Peter 3:3-4 says "Do not let your adornment be merely outward - arranging the hair, wearing gold, or putting on fine apparel - rather let it be the hidden person of the heart, with the incorruptible beauty of a gentle and quiet spirit, which is very precious in the sight of God." We are living in a society that is motivated by outer beauty rather than inward character. Women spend more money outwardly adorning themselves than focusing on the spiritual woman that will live forever. Yes, you should look your best because you are representing the King. However, if our lips are painted, but our mouths are gossipy and destructive; if our hair is done, but our thoughts are vindictive and jealous; if our feet are pedicured, but we walk in disobedience; if our nails are manicured and they only clasp together when I want something from God; and if our attire portrays God's temple in a seductive way (how much cleavage have you seen in the Church lately?), then if you were given a nickname descriptive of your character, would you be proud of it? We don't need an "Extreme Makeover" as much as we need an "Extreme Heart Takeover!"

The Lord is not as concerned with what we look like on the outside as He is about the attitude of our hearts. A gentle and quiet spirit is beauty that never decays as the outward body does. "Gentle" means to be "meek or humble" or it is just strength under control. "Quiet" describes the character of our action and reaction to our husband and life in general. This kind of beauty is precious to her husband as well as to the Lord.

Emotions play by no rules! I remember when a sister told me that she asked the Lord if He would turn His back so that she could hit her husband over the head with a frying pan. No! No! No! I, however, remember the times when I would have a pity party and would have to find a solitary place (have you been in the bathroom lately?) There I would cry and talk to the Lord, because my **heart** was hurting and I wanted to scream. **Psalm 6:6 "I am weary with my groaning; all night I make my bed swim; I drench my couch with my tears."** But, the Lord heard my cries.

> *Happiness is inward, and not outward; and so it does not depend on what we have, but on what we are.*
> *(Henry Van Dyke)*

Wrong Thinking + Wrong Feelings = Wrong Actions

When emotions are out of balance, there are some things we will automatically do. We **will** have a pity party. We **will** blame God for our circumstances. We **will** say "if You didn't allow me to be in this family, or marry this man, my life wouldn't have turned out like this." Sometimes we get angry with the Lord. **Yes, we get angry with God!** We say "Why are You allowing all of these things to happen to me when I am trying to live right." Emotions are real. We have to recognize that when they take control, it is sin. We have to call it what God calls it. **I John 1:9 says "If we confess our sins, He is faithful and just to forgive us our sins and to cleanse us from all unrighteousness."**

When I come to the end of my rope, God is there to take over.

Depression is one of those feelings that comes as a result of not handling or working through problems in a spiritual manner. It is a negative emotion due to self-defeating perceptions and appraisals. It is a feeling of hopelessness, despair, sadness and apathy. Depression can be caused by physical, mental, emotional, or spiritual problems and CHRISTIANS CAN SUFFER WITH DEPRESSION! We have to learn to handle our problems God's way if we want God's results! **Remember,** in trials we will grow or self-destruct, get better or become bitter, become a conqueror or we will be conquered by life.

Look around you and be distressed, look within you and be depressed, look to Jesus and be at rest.

Wrong emotions can also cause us to have a faith-doubt crisis. **Hebrews 11:1 says "Now faith is the substance of things hoped for, the evidence of things not seen."** Doubt causes our thinking to be divided within, not merely because of mental indecision, but an inner distrust in God. We can then become insensitive to His voice. **Hebrews 3:7-11 says " Therefore, as the Holy Spirit says: Today, if you will hear His voice, do not harden your hearts as in the rebellion, in the day of trial in the wilderness, where your fathers tested Me, tried Me, and saw My works forty years. Therefore, I was angry with that generation, and said, they always go astray in their hearts, and they have not known my ways, so I swore in My wrath, they shall not enter My rest."**

Today refers to your life at this moment, even while reading this book. God urges you to give attention to His voice "**right**

now!" God had promised to give rest to His people in the land of Canaan, but they rebelled against Him and an entire generation was prohibited from entering the Promised Land. God wants to give us spiritual rest, but when we go astray in our hearts, our trials then become bigger than our God.

Our lives are lived in seasons and restlessness is a by-product of the season of change. When the Lord begins to expand your border, He will stir up your nest to move you out of your comfort zone. I went through a faith-doubt crisis when I made the decision to change my church membership and became a founding member of a new church, Genesis Bible Fellowship Church in Baltimore, Maryland. Little did I know that this move would catapult me into the next level of women's ministry.

> *Faith is not belief without proof, but trust without reservation.*

Romans 8:26 says "Likewise the Spirit also helps our weaknesses. For we do not know what we should pray for as we ought, but the Spirit Himself makes intercession for us with groanings which cannot be uttered." Even in our pain and suffering, we must yield to the Holy Spirit. As we seek Him, He will control our thinking, thereby controlling our emotions. Sometimes our emotions make us see suffering as a personal attack from God. We think He doesn't care about who we are. We can even have a deep sense of loneliness and isolation. We may feel as though no one understands what we are going through or are suffering as we are. We have to remember that there is nothing new under the sun.

Therefore, in controlling your emotions you must:

> (1) Confess known sin.
> (2) Be real if you are angry with God.
> (3) Examine yourself and ask, "Why am I responding this way?"
> (4) Encourage your own heart by hoping in God.
> (5) Don't let feelings be your guide, just do what you are required to do.

Actions change feelings. We must learn to acknowledge feelings and then express them in a way that honors God. Work on your actions and the right feelings will follow. (**Pastor Wayne Cockrell**)

> *It isn't your position that makes you happy or unhappy, it's your disposition.*

Finding Fulfillment

Question: Are you stressed? If so, what stressful event has entered your life? How are you responding?

Challenge: Tell the Lord how you are feeling. Be real and say what's in your heart (remember He already knows). Now, yield to the Holy Spirit and your right actions will change your feelings.

The melting process is a heart matter. **Proverbs 3:5-6 says "Trust in the Lord with all your heart and lean not on your own understanding. In all of your ways acknowledge Him and He will direct your path."** What is the heart? The heart is the innermost center of man. It includes: (1) the center of feelings and affections (emotions); (2) the seat of conscience; (3) the choosing part of our being which is referred to as our will; (4) the mind which encompasses the thinking, intellectual part of our human spirit; and (5) the dwelling place of Christ, if you are born again. The heart is important because out of it springs the issues of life.

> *What lies behind us and what lies before us are tiny matters compared to what lies within us.*
> *(Ralph Waldo Emerson)*

In the Hebrew, the word **trust** means to "body slam" which is a wrestling term. It means to cling to the Lord no matter what happens; adhere to Him and never let go. The Lord wants us to do more then just "believe" that He can do what He says, but He wants us to literally "body-slam" onto Him and cleave with all of our strength. When the fiery trials are prevailing, God and God alone must be the object of our trust. We will either **trust** God or we won't. **(Proverbs for Easier Living, Jo Berry)**

> *Sometimes the Lord calms the storm; sometimes He lets the storm rage and calms His child.*

As Jacob wrestled with the LORD and would not let go until He blessed him, I also learned what it meant to wrestle with God. Raymond had always been an excellent provider, but after 10 years on a job, he became unemployed. As a man, I know that it impacted him. It also greatly impacted me because I had just started back to work on a part-time basis after being home for 9 years to raise my daughters. For three days I wrestled with the Lord and this brought about tension headaches because of my worry. After the third day, the Holy Spirit spoke to my heart and said "How long are you going to worry since you don't know how long this trial will last?" Well I knew that I had no idea, so I had to "body slam" and cling to the Lord in a way I never had. It was a year before Raymond returned to work and the Lord supplied all of our needs. (I was beginning to understand the meaning of Jehovah Jireh - The Lord my Provider!)

Yet this was only the beginning of job instabilities that continued over the years for Raymond. God would use this particular type of trial to teach me to cleave and trust Him as my ultimate provider. After I became a widow in 2004, the Lord continued to supply my needs through my part-time job and my ministry. However, my part-time position was terminated on Thursday, May 31, 2007, but God had financial provisions in place on Monday, June 4, 2007. Reflecting back on what the Lord had taught me, I now **trust** the Lord Who has blessed and provided for me through full time ministry. **BUT GOD!**

> *If the roots are deep and strong, the tree needn't worry about the wind.*

Pastor Wayne Cockrell gives these practical considerations when being refined:

(a) Focus on God's sovereignty, power, and mercy. **Psalms 3, 4, 5, 6.**

> *The greatest act of faith is when man decides he is not God.*

(b) Remember **II Corinthians 1:3 4:** "Blessed be the God and Father of our Lord Jesus Christ, the Father of mercies and God of all comfort, who comforts us in all our tribulation, that we may be able to comfort those who are in any trouble, with the comfort with which we ourselves are comforted by God."

(1) God allows problems.

(2) God is with us in our problems.

(3) God has mercy on us in our problems.

(4) God comforts us in our problems.

(5) God prepares us to comfort others.

Character is not made in crisis, it is only exhibited.

(c) Remember that everyone has conflicts in life. **I Corinthians 10:13** "No temptation has overtaken you except such as is common to man; but God is faithful, who will not allow you to be tempted beyond what you are able, but with the temptation will also make the way of escape, that you may be able to bear it."

It's not whether you get knocked down; it's whether you get up again.

(Vince Lombardi)

(d) Be aware that every conflict has the potential to change you into a Peter or Judas. **Proverbs 13:20** "He who walks with wise men will be wise, but the companion of fools will be destroyed."

A pessimist is one who makes difficulties of his opportunities; an optimist is one who makes opportunities of his difficulties.

(Reginald Mansell)

(e) There is a right way and a wrong way to handle each problem. Proverbs 14:12 "There is a way that seems right to a man, but its end is the way of death."

> *Never miss an opportunity to make others happy;*
> *even if you have to leave them alone in order to do it.*

(f) You must choose how you will handle your problem. Psalm 37:5 "Commit your way to the Lord, trust also in Him, and He shall bring it to pass."

> *Experience is what you get when you don't get what you want.*
>
> *(Dan Stanford)*

In the refining process, the Lord was softening my heart. He also continued to open doors for me to share the Word of God with women. Sometimes I felt so unworthy to be used by the Lord when I knew that I didn't have it altogether. Yet, I was becoming real and touchable.

Many times, we hide behind masks pretending to be what we aren't. We are, also, afraid of what people will think when they know the "real" you. Sad to say, the Church is not always the safest place to reveal the real you. The Bible says "But, God has chosen the foolish things of the world to put to shame the wise, and God has chosen the weak things of the world to put to shame the things that are mighty; and the base things of the world and the things despised God has chosen, and the things which are not, to bring to nothing the things that are, that no flesh should glory in His presence." (I Corinthians 1:27-29)

As our lives are being purified by the Lord, Bible reading alone won't solve our problems. God says in Philippians 2:12

"Therefore, my beloved, as you have always obeyed, not as in my presence only, but now much more in my absence, work out your own salvation with fear and trembling." James 1:5 also says "If any of you lacks wisdom, let him ask of God, Who gives to all liberally and without reproach, and it will be given to him." Trials produce character not only by the pain of the process, but more importantly by the application of the Word of God. God will work in us the will, but we have to work it out through obedience. You and I have to ask for wisdom if we are to come through God's melting process.

When I think of the wisdom it takes to mature through this melting process, I also think of the wisdom it takes to build healthy relationships as you grow in Christ. The scope of womanhood encompasses many facets of life: singleness, marriage, mothering, divorce and widowhood. Our continued education, new career choices and church fellowships offer a great diversity of circumstances to develop friendships. Research suggests that the emotional intimacy and the give-and-take of emotional support that women give each other are of great value to female relationships.

> *Everyone has an invisible sign hanging from his neck saying, "Make me feel important!"*

The Lord had blessed me with a wonderful relationship with my Mom and my sisters Brenda and Kathy, but, being the oldest, I always found myself counseling, discipling, or encouraging. Thus, Christ began to develop women friendships that provided me with other valuable lessons as I grew in Christ.

There was a season in my marriage when I was going through some inner struggles and I knew that I could not share my real heart issues with just anyone. However, God was building an intimate friendship. For one year, my girlfriend Glenda Spence and I shared heart issues. She was single and I was married, and although we were struggling with different issues, our hearts were hurting at the same time. This kind of scenario (we would go through similar circumstances at the same time) would encompass our lasting friendship of over 30 years.

As I expanded my friendships with women, God was providing experience in these relationships that would eventually prepare me for my own women's ministry. In 1989, Cheryl Torain Ministries began which encompassed my singing and speaking. I also started the women's ministry at my church and have served in this capacity for over 20 years. One thing that I am sure of, you should be led by the Holy Spirit to lead a women's ministry, if you are going to endure. We can be very fickle, moody and jealous. Therefore, relationships can be risky, but the dividends far outweigh the risks. Women friendships provide a reservoir of untapped God-given strength, support, love and encouragement.

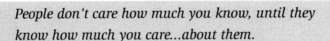

People don't care how much you know, until they know how much you care...about them.

Four levels of friendships are generally recognized: an **acquaintance** is someone with whom you have occasional contact; a **casual** friend is someone you work with or see at church or a meeting on a regular basis; a **close** friend is someone with whom you actively plan frequent contact with and share positive feelings and joys, as well as frustrations and burdens, and an **intimate** friend is one with whom you have open honesty and mutual commitment. An intimate friendship is rare and special and takes a lot of time and work, but the rewards are tremendous. (**Frank Minirth, M.D**)

Dr. Minirth considers the following suggestions for developing friendships:

    a. Like yourself first.

    b. Look for experiences and activities you enjoy. In short, have fun!

    c. Cultivate the ability to see and enjoy the uniqueness of each individual you encounter.

    d. Smile.

    e. Encourage others to talk about their lives and feelings.

    f. Be a good listener.

    g. Watch for opportunities to celebrate their successes.

    h. Develop empathy for others. Empathy is the ability to comprehend another person's emotions and attitudes. Help your friends through their problems.

    i. Make a commitment to loyalty.

    j. Learn to forgive each other and work through conflicts.

    k. Be honest. Tell the truth, even when it hurts.

    l. Minister together. Share a common goal to serve Christ.

Finding Fulfillment

Question: Many of us have casual and close friendships, but do you have an intimate friend?

Challenge: Do a study on the friendships of women. Remember, to have a friend, you must first be "friendly."

Friendships also involve what I call the "Daniel" experience where you learn that Jesus must first become your best friend. The Lord clearly spoke to my heart that I was now to start walking alone. My familiar networks would have a different priority in my life. As Daniel was taken from the safe environment of his home and family to a foreign land to walk alone, God was now teaching me the power of His presence. My life verse has become **I Corinthians 5:9 "Therefore, I make it my aim, whether absent or present to be well pleasing to Him."**

The Lord is so specific in the plans He has for us. **Proverbs 19:21 says "There are plans in a man's heart, nevertheless the LORD's counsel - that will stand."** I have always had leadership abilities even as a little girl, but now they were being manifested in the ministry God had given me. I traveled alone to speaking and singing engagements and He always protected me, even without a **cell phone!** What a privilege and honor it is to serve the Lord.

> *The secret of contentment is the realization that life is a gift not a right.*

During this "Daniel" experience, He also taught me "how not to fear." In 1991, after celebrating my birthday with some friends, I returned home and was robbed by gunpoint in front of my house, **BUT GOD!** Ten years later, I was again robbed by gunpoint in front of my home, **BUT GOD!** In the beginning of 2001, I had two car accidents and then totaled my car on September 11, 2001 at the same time others in New York at the World Trade Center were ushered into eternity, **BUT GOD!** The Lord was training me to have a level of trust in Him that assured me that my life was in His hands and nothing could harm me or my life be taken until His appointed time. **II Corinthians 5:10 "For we must all appear** before the judgment seat of Christ, that each one may receive the things done in the body, according to what he has done, whether good or bad."

As I cultivated my spiritual gift of encouragement and ministered to others, I remembered many times in the melting process what David said in **I Samuel 30:6b** "But David strengthened himself in the LORD his God." Even when my heart was aching, I was learning the value of encouraging my own heart.

There was a group of women doing a Bible study on the book of Malachi. As they were studying chapter three, they came across verse three which says "**He will sit as a refiner and purifier of silver.**" This verse puzzled the women and they wondered what this statement meant about the character and nature of God. One of the women offered to find out about the process of refining silver and get back to the group at their next study.

That week this woman called up a silversmith and made an appointment to watch him work. She didn't mention anything about the reason for her interest in silver beyond sharing her curiosity about the process of refining silver. As she watched the silversmith, he held a piece of silver in the middle of the fire and let it heat up. He explained that in refining silver, one needed to hold the silver in the middle of the fire where the flames were hottest in order to burn away all the impurities. The woman thought about God holding us in such a hot spot. Then she thought again about the verse, "**He sits as a refiner and purifier of silver.**" She asked the silversmith if it was true that he had to sit there in front of the fire the whole time the silver was being refined. The man said yes, he not only had to sit there holding the silver in place, but he had to keep his eyes on the silver the entire time it was in the fire. If the silver were left even a moment too long in the flames, it would be destroyed. The woman was silent for a moment. Then she asked the silversmith, *How do you know when the silver is fully* *refined?* He smiled at her and answered, *Oh, that's easy – when I see my image in it.*

God was beginning to see His image in my life. My pain was becoming my praise and purpose! My tests were confirming my testimony and my suffering was producing service! Learning to thank God for the pain of my heart and the darkness of my soul truly brought me out to "rich fulfillment." I now read **Psalm 66:10-12** as follows:

> "For You, O God, have tested ME; You have refined ME as silver is refined. You brought ME into the net; You laid affliction on MY back.
>
> You have caused men to ride over MY head; I went through fire and through water; but You brought ME out to rich fulfillment."

Color Me A Woman of God: Melt Me!!

Color Me a Woman of God:
Mold Me
(Expandable Clay in the Master's Hands)

THE POTTER'S HOUSE

To the Potter's house I went down one day
And watched Him while molding the vessels of clay
And many a wonderful lesson I drew
As I noted the process the clay went through.

Trampled and broken, downtrodden and rolled
To render more plastic and fit for the mold
How like the clay that is human, I thought
When in heavenly hands to perfection brought.

For self must be cast as the dust at His feet
Before it is ready for service made meet
And pride must be broken, and self will be lost
All laid on the altar, **whatever the cost.**

But lo! By and by, a delicate vase
Of wonderful beauty and exquisite grace
Was it once the vile clay? Ah, yes; yet how strange
The Potter has wrought so marvelous a change!

Not a trace of the earth, nor mark of the clay
The fires of the furnace have burned them away
Wondrous skill of the Potter - the praise is His due
In whose hands to perfection and beauty it grew;

Thus with souls lying still, content in God's hand,
That do not His power of working withstand
They are molded and fitted, a treasure to hold;
Vile clay now transformed into purest of gold.

Vile clay being transformed into the image of Christ, how awesome a thought! That's what I am as He is molding me on a daily basis. **Romans 8:29 "For whom He did foreknow He also predestined to be conformed to the image of His Son."** Christ is the image in which our attitude and character should be molded.

> *Reputation is made in a moment: character is built in a lifetime.*

There are two general types of clay, based on how the substance reacts when mixed with water. *Expandable clay* swells when water is added to it. Expandable clay can absorb so much water that the clay itself becomes a liquid. *Nonexpandable clay* becomes soft but not liquid when mixed with water. *Nonexpandable clay* is used in making pottery, bricks, and tile. For example, pottery makers mold moist clay into almost any shape and bake it in hot ovens called *kilns*. Heat removes the water from the clay, which becomes permanently hard and cannot be softened by adding water to it.

Jesus Christ is the "living water" who desires to mold us into His image. The Samaritan woman of **John 4** drank from the fountain of living water and was transformed. As we absorb "the water of the Word," we become *expandable clay* and channels for others to drink. But if the heat of trials absorbs the "water of the Word," we become *nonexpendable clay* and hardened.

Jesus encountered the Samaritan woman and had initially asked her for water because He was thirsty. However, the conversation was to make her aware of her need of Him, the "living water." The issue wasn't theology, but a personal relationship. When He announced that He was the Messiah, she believed and immediately left her water pot to share the Good News with others. Christ had transformed her thinking to see both herself and Him more clearly. She initially had been ashamed and uncertain, and had isolated herself from her neighbors. Now the *expandable clay* hurried to tell others about Jesus and became a conduit of salvation for many. Cleansed and transformed, she focused on Christ rather than herself.

> *It's good to be a Christian and know it, but it's better to be a Christian and show it!*

There are things that we can change about ourselves, but there are also things that are unchangeable. The unchangeables (you know what they are) become marks of ownership that glorifies God. Because we are fearfully and wonderfully made, we must understand that our self worth comes from the Lord. The Samaritan woman was so hungry for love and a relationship that she welcomed anyone who would have her - even with no commitment involved.

False Beliefs + False Thinking + False Emotions = False Actions

We must change our past thinking process if we are going to grow into Christlikeness. **Romans 12:1-2 says "I beseech you brethren, by the mercies of God, that you present your bodies a living sacrifice, holy, acceptable to God, which is your reasonable service. And do not be conformed to this world, but be transformed by the renewing of your mind, that you may prove what is that good and perfect will of God."** If our experiences, environments, and educational attitudes are negative, then the beliefs about ourselves, others and life will be on the negative side. By renewing the mind with God's Word, we develop new beliefs, which become safety filters to strain our thoughts, emotions and actions.

God uses **faith** to integrate this new potential into our new belief system. We are now enabled to think differently about ourselves from God's perspective. **II Corinthians 10:5 "casting down arguments and every high thing that exalts itself against the knowledge of God, bring every thought into captivity to the obedience of Christ."**

God's Words + Right Thinking + Right Emotions = Right Actions

A bridge is now developed from our old perspective to our new potential. God desires that we have a biblical view of who we are. Therefore, we should:

a) Be honest about who we are at a deeper level (God is a discerner of the thoughts and intents of the heart); just be REAL.
b) Find one or two **spiritual** people with whom you can be transparent.
c) Accept God's truth and experience healing.
d) Remember that growth towards maturity is a life time journey.
(Pastor Wayne Cockrell)

We are in an age where there is a mass stampede for power, titles, recognition, status and prestige among God's women. These things do not authenticate our personhood. Feminism stresses that my personal significance is according to opportunity for personal fulfillment, but God says, "**He who loses his life for my sake will find it.**"

Acceptance of Who I Am

False Concept: Self Worth = Performance + Other's Opinions

Acceptance is when we allow another person's behavior to control our pattern of living that determines our self worth. Low self-esteem is an instrument used by Satan to hinder us from meeting our full potential in Christ. It can come from a lack of: love, acceptance, laughter/fun, sense of worth, attention, friendship, forgiveness or affirmation.

Remember, no one can make you feel inferior without your consent.

Genesis 29:31 says **"When the LORD saw that Leah was unloved, He opened her womb; but Rachel was barren."** Rachel and Leah were sisters whose lives were closely intertwined. They were the daughters of Laban, and both were married to Jacob, the son of their Uncle Isaac. It is clear from Genesis that Jacob loved Rachel, and considered her his primary wife, while he "hated Leah" (that is, rejected Leah's claim to a primary position even though he had wed her first). The Bible in no way suggests or teaches polygamy. This complex relationship created extreme pain and competition for each of the women, and undoubtedly for Jacob as well.

> *Life can seem bleak indeed when the most important relationship in our experience turns out to be marred at the onset by deception or disappointment.*

Leah kept looking for love, acceptance, and approval from Jacob, and she was continually disappointed until she reoriented her life towards God. We see this in the names she gave her sons. When the first son was born, Leah named him Reuben ("See, a son!"), but Jacob's lack of love for her did not change. Her second son was called Simeon ("Heard"), because the Lord had heard that she was unloved. Despite the gift of children, she continued to experience rejection from Jacob.

When a third son was born, Leah called him Levi ("attached"), believing that Jacob would become attached to her, but again she was disappointed. With the birth of her fourth son, Leah finally began to look away from her husband for love, and to look to the Lord. She named her fourth son Judah ("Praise"). **(Women of the Bible)**

> *Success in marriage is more than finding the right person, it's becoming the right person.*

In 1987, when I hit the BIG "40," I was frustrated. Even though I had the empty nest syndrome, my marriage was not what I thought it should be at this point in my life. I whined and cried for 6 months about "ME, MYSELF, and I." Have you even gotten tired of just praying for yourself? Well, I did! So I had to get over it!! We are *expandable clay* in the Master's Hand. I, too, had to understand that the "hole" in my heart and my ultimate satisfaction was not to be in my husband, but could only be found in Jesus Christ. He alone is the one stable source in our existence. It would be 17 years later that the Lord would bring to fruition His marvelous plan.

> *The most important step towards joy in a loveless marriage is to change our focus from what we do not have to what we do have.*

Leah's character and her relationship with God did develop. While God didn't change Jacob's heart, God did love Leah and blessed her with seven children. Even in our mess, circumstances or hurts, Christ can make something beautiful out of our pain. Our misery becomes our ministry and our pain truly can produce "Praise!"

Finding Fulfillment

Question: Leah's competition was a man, what is yours? A job, a sport, the ministry, etc.?

Challenge: Return to your "first love." Renew your intimacy with Jesus. Think about Him, talk to Him, adore Him, praise Him, and worship Him!!

FOUR "DOWN-CASTERS"

"Down-casters" are those factors in life experiences which destroy self-esteem and promote the development of a negative self-concept. They are:

1. **Discouraging Comments - Jeremiah 9:8 "Their tongue is an arrow shot out; it speaks deceit; one speaks peaceably to his neighbor with his mouth, but in his heart he lies in wait."**

Jeremiah was challenging Judah that they would go through the fiery furnace of affliction to remove the dross because of their sins. The prophet was emphasizing that the tongues of God's people that had dealt death and deceit was second nature to them. Even when their conversation appeared to be cordial, their hearts were scheming to ensnare their neighbors.

It is not productive to spend time around individuals who discourage us from believing in ourselves and in what Christ can do in and through us. However, certain relationships do not afford us a change in environment, so we are constantly challenged to have the right attitude of heart where we are.

Sometimes in the Church, the greatest pain can come from those who are unguarded in their thoughts, thereby, speaking what is really in their hearts. Some of my greatest pain has come from things said about me that eventually got back to me. Very insecure people will many times be used as an instrument of the enemy to discourage you and the enemy will make sure you find out. As a young believer, I was very sensitive to negative criticism, but the Lord had to toughen me through the years if I was going to be used as an instrument of His grace and especially with women. Even Joseph was discouraged and sold into slavery by his brothers, exiled to Egypt and eventually put in prison on false accusations. But what they meant for evil, God meant for good. He was eventually elevated from prison to the palace in one day, yet it took 13 years for the molding process.

The Lord was molding and teaching me how to respond correctly to negativism and discouraging comments. Sometimes the Lord challenged me to lovingly confront individuals and other times He handled it His way. I'm learning how much better it is to let the Lord fight your battles. Someone has said that we should take the negative criticism, sift it for what is true, make the necessary changes and toss the rest. I've learned that it really makes your enemies and Satan angry when they can't control you by their negativism and insecurities.

Before I came to know Christ as my Savior, I never sang or knew that I could sing. As a new believer, I joined the choir and realized that God had given me the talent to sing and I was encouraged to develop my talent by my music director. My voice range was very high and undeveloped. I later found out that someone made fun of my voice. Even though it got back to me and it hurt, music ministered to my soul in such a way that I chose not to listen to those negative or discouraging comments. I have, therefore, been blessed to have produced three CD's (**He Cares for You, 1989; From My Heart to You Lord, 1997, and Prepared to Praise, 2004**) that have encouraged people around the world. God's maturity in my ministry of music was demonstrated on my last CD "Prepared to Praise" because I was inspired by the Lord to write the words to 11 of the 15 selections. **Glory to God!**

Be more concerned with what God thinks about you than what people think about you.

My commitment to the Lord Jesus Christ brought about negative criticism many times from my husband, Raymond. **Proverbs 18:21 says "Death and life are in the power of the tongue, and those who love it will eat its fruit."** When he would criticize me, I would sometimes run to the Word of God and let the Word reassure me as to who I was in Christ. However, sometimes I retaliated with negative criticism. Hurting people hurt people!

A critical spirit is like poison ivy – it only takes a little contact to spread its poison.

People may doubt what you say, but they will always believe what you do. The Lord challenged me through the Word in **Proverbs 15:1 "A soft answer turns away wrath, but a harsh word stirs up anger. The tongue of the wise uses knowledge rightly, but the mouth of fools pours forth foolishness."** As I used my tongue rightly, Raymond saw the changes in my attitude and changed the way he responded to me. Obedience is always better than sacrifice.

Stack every bit of criticism between two layers of praise.

2. Unfair Comparisons – II Corinthians 10:12 "For we dare not class ourselves or compare ourselves with those who commend themselves. But they, measuring themselves by themselves, and comparing themselves among themselves, are not wise."

David, a man after God's own heart, experienced an unfair comparison. As David and King Saul were returning home from slaughtering the Philistines, the women came out to sing and dance with joy and musical instruments. They sang in **I Samuel 18: 7-8a "Saul has slain his thousands, and David his ten thousands. Then Saul was very angry, and the saying displeased him…"** The Hebrew word translated "angry" means "to burn within" and the Hebrew word for "displeased" means "inner turmoil." As Saul did a slow burn, his stomach turned. Saul's self talk led him to "look at David from that day on" with suspicion. Thus, suspicion was fueled by jealousy that grew to hate.

Paul's challenge to the Corinthians was to show humility when he refused to compare himself with others, or engage in self-promotion. His only personal concern was what the Lord thought of him. When we compare ourselves with others we often need certain people to validate us. When that doesn't happen, we tend to feel ineffective.

We have to learn to operate in the sphere of our God given influence and giftedness which will meet all of our needs for success and achievement.

> *The Lord can do great things through those who don't care who gets the credit.*

As I grew in Christ, I had to accept my own uniqueness and try not to compare my singing or teaching style to someone else's. Sometime others will compare you to someone else, but we should always "esteem others better than ourselves." The flesh always wants to be exalted, but it's the humble who God exalts in His due time.

Remember that God has set each one of us in the body as

it pleased Him. He gave diversity of gifts, diversity of services to exercise our gifts, and diversity of ways our gifts would be manifested. There is only "one" you!! Therefore, when God created you, He threw away the mold.

> *I don't know the secret to success, but the key to failure is to try to please everyone.*
>
> *(Bill Cosby)*

3. Negative Thinking - Romans 12:2 "And do not be conformed to this world, but be transformed by the renewing of your mind..."

In order to think right, we have to be transformed (metamorphosized) by the renewing of our minds. We have to change the way we think now that we are in Christ. The word "transformed" denotes that on a daily basis what is going on inwardly in our hearts is what should be displayed outwardly in our actions. Let's stop the masquerade! This world system is already infiltrated by satan who infects us with ungodly beliefs and values through television, the internet, ungodly literature, and a world system that is totally against God. I John 2:15-16 "Do not love the world or the things in the world. If anyone loves the world, the love of the Father is not in him. For all that is in the world – the lust of the flesh, the lust of the eyes, and the pride of life – is not of the Father but is of the world." Remember, if experiences, environments, education, and attitudes are negative, then beliefs about oneself, others and life will be on the negative side. Transformation is from the inside out because God is working in us to eventually work through us.

Even in the Church we see these ungodly beliefs and values expressed in many ways. We see this mindset in how we serve the Lord through our ministry (we give the Lord whatever is left over); we see it in our lack of commitment to truth; we see it in how we treat one another in our fellowships, and we see it in the unbiblical choices we make. Therefore, by renewing our minds through the Word of God, we begin to think like the Bible. This kind of transformation can only occur as the Holy Spirit controls our minds through consistent study and meditation of Scripture. The renewed mind is one saturated with, controlled by, and empowered by the Word of God.

> *Language is the expression of thought. Every time you speak, your mind is on parade.*

4. Unreasonable Expectations - Philippians 3:14 "I press toward the goal for the prize of the upward call of God in Christ Jesus."

Paul uses the analogy of a runner to describe the Christian's growth. The believer has not reached the goal of Christlikeness, but like the runner in a race, he must continue to pursue it. When we get to heaven and into God's presence, we will receive the prize which has been an unattainable goal in this earthly life. (**MacArthur Study Bible**) However, unrealistic or unreasonable expectations in this life will make you feel "locked in" to someone else's self image only to eventually weaken and destroy any positive concept you may have. Many of us place unrealistic expectations on others.

The Lord Jesus has given each one of us spiritual gifts in which to edify the body of Christ and give Him glory. The discovery and development of our spiritual gifts will be a signpost directing us to God's will for our lives. When we understand areas that we are gifted, responsible and empowered to do, we will not be so quick to fulfill the purposes of others instead of the purposes of God.

> *The mighty oak was once a little nut that stood its ground.*

Finding Fulfillment

Question: Which particular "down-caster" is affecting your walk with Christ?

Challenge: Identify it, memorize a Scripture of victory and then apply the Word to your life.

The middle letter of sin is "I" and the middle letter of pride is "I." We can have low self esteem, and we can also think too highly of ourselves. **J. Oswald Sanders** says "There is nothing more distasteful to God than self-conceit. This first and fundamental sin in essence aims at enthroning self at the expense of God... Pride is a sin of whose presence its victim is least conscious...If we are honest, when we measure ourselves by the life of our Lord who humbled Himself even to death on a cross, we cannot but be overwhelmed with the tawdriness and shabbiness, and even the vileness, of our hearts."

> *Pride is the only disease known to man that makes everyone sick except the person who has it.*
>   *(Buddy Robinson)*

Four "Up-Lifters"

If I were to draw a caricature that would symbolize the millions of adults with low self-esteem, I would depict a bowed, weary traveler. Over his shoulder I would place the end of a mile-long chain to which is attached tons of scrap iron, old tires and garbage of all types. Each piece of junk is inscribed with the details of some humiliation – a failure – an embarrassment – a rejection from the past. He would let go of the chain and free himself from the heavy load which immobilizes and exhausts him, but he is somehow convinced that it must be dragged throughout life...Paralyzed by its weight, he plods onward, digging a furrow in the good earth as he goes. You can free yourself from the weight of the chain if you will but turn it loose. **(James Dotson, Hide and Seek)**

There are some specific factors in life experiences which help build self-esteem and promote the development of a positive self concept. They are:

1. **Accept God's Purpose - Ephesians 1:11 "In Him also we have obtained an inheritance, being predestined according to the purpose of Him who works all things according to the counsel of His will..."**

Christ is the source of our divine inheritance. Before the earth was formed, God sovereignly determined that every elect sinner, however vile, useless and deserving of death - by trusting in Christ would be made righteous. The word translated "works" is the same one in which "energy," "energetic," and "energize" are derived. When God created the world, He gave it sufficient energy to begin immediately to operate as He had planned. It was not simply ready to function, but was created functioning. As God works out His plan according "to the counsel of His will," He energizes every believer with the power necessary for his spiritual completion. (MacArthur Study Bible)

We were made by God and for God's purposes and pleasure. I remember the night when I accepted the Lord Jesus Christ into my heart. The blinders fell from my eyes and I felt a spiritual energy because I knew that I was forgiven. I am an optimist by nature with a very outgoing and energetic personality, so my salvation added to me a new level of sufficient energy to function. Saints have told me that I am sometimes like "the energizer bunny" for Christ, even at my age!

> *God never asks about our ability or our inability –*
> *just our availability.*

2. **Know and Do God's Will - Philippians 2:13 "...for it is God Who works in you both to will and to do for His good pleasure."**

We are told to work out not for our salvation, because the Lord is the One who produces the good works and spiritual fruit in our lives. As we abide in Him and His words abide in us, the Holy Spirit works through us to will and to do. God then energizes our desires and actions. The "will" is not based on emotions, but the intent to fulfill a purpose. Therefore, we are enabled to do what satisfies Him. Just as the Lord Jesus said "not My will, but Thy will be done," we too should mature in saying "not my will Lord, but Thy will be done."

> *To know the will of God is the greatest knowledge, to*
> *find the will of God is the greatest discovery, and to do*
> *the will of God is the greatest achievement.*
> *(George W. Truett)*

3. Involve Your Life in the Lives of Other People   Matthew 20:28 "Just as the Son of Man did not come to be served, but to serve and give His life a ransom for many."

Christ and the disciples constantly met the needs of other people. We can stabilize our own hearts during times of difficulty by serving others and then find that our service has brought us a sense of satisfaction and emotional healing. During Jesus' time, the Gentile leaders dictated by using carnal power and authority. We as believers, however, are to do just the opposite – we lead by being servants and giving ourselves away to others, as Jesus did. I love the ministry of service that God has called me to and putting on the apron of servanthood is a must for every believer in Jesus Christ. If you have deep heart issues against God's people and avoid serving because of what a few have done to you, then check your heart. Maybe it's you and not "those Christians." Jesus said in John 13:35 "By this all will know that you are My disciples, if you have love for one another."

People may doubt what you say, but they will always believe what you do.

4. Stay on God's Timetable – Psalm 90:12 "So teach us to number our days that we may apply our hearts to wisdom."

In light of the brevity of life, God says that we are to evaluate how wisely we use time. There are no such things as accidents, incidents, or anything that is wasted because God is sovereign and everything is on His timetable. The Bible has a familiar saying throughout the Old Testament "and it came to pass" which testifies that what God says **"will come to pass."** So as we understand our purpose and value in the plan of God, let us:

a. **Work Hard – Philippians 4:13 "I can do all things through Christ Who strengthens me."** Paul uses a Greek word that means "to be strong" or "to have strength." He had strength to withstand "all things" including both difficulty and prosperity in the material world. Because believers are in Christ, God infuses them His strength to sustain them until they receive some provision. **(MacArthur Study Bible)**

    We as Christians can become lazy in this journey. We say "Let someone else do it," "This task is too hard and will take too long" or "I can do it tomorrow." God has called and equipped us with everything we need to deal with life. When we waste God-given opportunities, we will lack contentment and fulfillment. If we are not faithful in the "little things," why should God trust us with more to mess up or complain about? It is going to cost us something to run this Christian race, so continue to be strong.

    When you kill time, remember that it has no resurrection.

b. **Persevere – I Corinthians 15:58 "Therefore, be steadfast, unmovable, always abounding in the work of the Lord for you know that your labor is not in vain in the Lord."** No matter how difficult it is or how long it is, God's timing makes it all worthwhile. Calvin Coolidge said "PRESS ON. Nothing in the world can take the place of persistence. Talent will not; nothing is more common than unsuccessful individuals with talent. Genius will not; unrewarded genius is almost a proverb. Education will not; the world is full of educated derelicts. Persistence and determination alone are omnipotent."

Abraham **pressed on** to receive the "son of promise;" Ruth **pressed on** to know the True and Living God that positioned her to be in the lineage of the Lord Jesus Christ; Mary of Bethany **pressed on** by choosing to sit at the feet of Jesus, thereby, being prepared for His upcoming death; and many, many more testify of the perseverance of the saints. But the ultimate demonstration of perseverance was our Lord and Savior Jesus Christ who **pressed all the way to Calvary for you and I. Oh what LOVE!!**

Live today to the fullest. Remember it's the first day of the rest of your life.

c. Be Patient with the Process – Colossians 1:11 "...**strengthen with all might, according to His glorious power, for all patience and longsuffering with joy...**" The process is never comfortable, but the end results far outweigh the pain of the process. Patience and longsuffering refer to the attitude one has during trials. "Patience" looks more at enduring difficult circumstances, while "longsuffering" looks at enduring difficult people. As I reflect on the 32 years of being in an unequally yoked marriage, any disappointment or hurt is swallowed up by the intimacy and sweet fellowship I have developed with the Lord.

The only preparation for tomorrow is the right use of today.

Finding Fulfillment

Question: Are you using God's time wisely? If not, why not? Who or what is consuming His time or agenda?

Challenge: Begin "today" to put things in proper perspective.Matthew 6:33 says "Seek first the Kingdom of God and His righteousness and all these things shall be added to you."

Color Me a Woman of God: Mold Me!!

Color Me a Woman of God:
Fill Me
(Room for Nothing More)

T HE Apostle Paul tells us to live victoriously and to avoid the excesses of the flesh. Moody once illustrated this truth as follows: "Tell me," he said to his audience, "how can I get the air out of this glass?" One man said, "Suck it out with a pump." Moody replied, "That would create a vacuum and shatter the glass." After many impossible suggestions, Moody smiled, picked up a pitcher of water and filled the glass. "There," he said, "all the air is now removed." He then went on to show that victory in the Christian life is not by sucking out a sin here and there, but rather by being filled with the Spirit.

Ephesians 5:18 says "And do not be drunk with wine which is dissipation; but be filled with the Spirit..." Paul was speaking mainly here about the drunken orgies commonly associated with many pagan worship ceremonies of that day. They were supposed to induce some ecstatic communion with the deities. He, however, challenges the believer to have true communion with God not by drunkenness, but by the filling of the Holy Spirit. Paul is not speaking of the Holy Spirit's indwelling or baptism because these take place at the moment of salvation. He is rather giving us a command to live continually under the **influence** of the Holy Spirit by letting the Word control us. (**The MacArthur Study Bible**)

It is only after being broken, melted, and molded am I in a position to now want the Holy Spirit to fill or control me. The word "fill" in Webster's Dictionary means "to put something into until there is room for nothing more." My body, my mind, my emotions, my will, should be places that I want Him to fill until "**there is room for nothing more.**"

> *The world wants your best, but God wants your all.*

The Holy Spirit is such a Gentleman. He never forces us to do anything, but gives us the privilege to cooperate with Him. As we live in the conscious presence of the Lord Jesus Christ and let the Word dominate our thinking, we will give freedom to the Holy Spirit to do in us what He desires. Yet as I continue to grow in Christ, the war still rages within – "**For the flesh lusts against the Spirit, and the Spirit against the flesh; and these are contrary to one another, so that you do not do the things you wish.**" (**Galatians 5: 16-17**)

Being filled is the same as "walking" in the Spirit. The Greek word translated "walk" indicates continuous action, or a habitual lifestyle. As we obey the simple commands of God's Word, we progress in our spiritual life, thereby, demonstrating the Spirit's control. The "flesh" part of me which includes my body, mind, will and emotions will always be subject to sin, but the Holy Spirit Who lives in me can now give me the power to please God. As you walk your talk by being filled, your unbelieving mate without a word may be won by your conduct.

> *You can't fill an empty bucket with a dry well.*

Jesus Christ in His humanity was "filled" with the Holy Spirit and He is our example. The Scripture says **"Then Jesus, being filled with the Holy Spirit, returned from the Jordan and was led by the Spirit into the wilderness..." (Luke 4:1)** As Jesus launched His public ministry, He demonstrated that a new life was possible. Jesus showed His own freedom from the inadequacies and the sin which traps you and me. Remember **"For we do not have a High Priest who cannot sympathize with our weaknesses, but was in all points tempted as we are, yet without sin." (Hebrews 4:15).** He understands, He knows, and He proves that freedom is possible as we allow the Holy Spirit to control us. Christ was tempted with "the lust of the flesh" **(Luke 4:2-3)**, "the lust of the eyes" **(Luke 4:8-9)**, and "the pride of life" **(Luke 4:5-6)**, and so will we. My mind can not grasp the depth of the temptation that the Lord went through to identify with me. After fasting for 40 days (I struggle with a few hours), and being physically weakened, He did not seek strength from the power and privilege of His Deity, but from the Holy Spirit. He was subject to hunger and needs as we are, yet He met every temptation in His human nature by the **Word of God.**

> *When you flee temptations, don't leave a forwarding address.*

As we become *expandable clay*, we provide the Holy Spirit the opportunity to "influence" us so that He can accomplish everything in our lives that He has ordained for us. Many times we resist because we think that we have better control of our lives, or we know what's best for us, or we have already mapped things out. No, it is not our way! "Be filled" is a command and it is to be done on a continuous day by day, moment by moment basis throughout our Christian journey.

When we resist being controlled by the Holy Spirit, we allow the enemy the opportunity to build "strongholds." A stronghold is a mindset that is contrary to Scripture. When this mindset is not corrected by the Word of God, tormentors enter into our hearts. These tormentors could be depression, fear, worry, envy, perversion, insecurity and other destructive emotions that are allowed by God to bring us to repentance. Yet when we confess this mindset as sin, find nourishment from the Word of God and seek to be filled with the Holy Spirit, we can be delivered.

Oswald Chambers in **My Utmost for His Highest** says, "We should not be a channel, but a fountain. Being filled and the sweetness of a vital relationship with Jesus will flow out of the saint as lavishly as it is imparted to him. If you find your life is not flowing out as it should, you are to blame; something has obstructed the flow. Keep right at the Source – the Holy Spirit. We are to be centers through which Jesus can flow as rivers of living water in blessing to everyone. Some of us are like the Dead Sea, always taking in but never giving out because we are not rightly related to the Lord Jesus."

Choice, not chance, determines human destiny.

Finding Fulfillment

Question: Is there a destructive emotion obstructing the control of the Holy Spirit? Is your life a fountain of living water or the Dead Sea?
Challenge: Confess and surrender this heart issue to the Lord. Begin to yield so that the Holy Spirit can fill you for today's walk.

It has been said that "**A Word-filled Christian is a Spirit-filled**

Christian." The evidence is seen in Colossians 3:16, "Let the Word of Christ dwell in you richly in all wisdom, teaching and admonishing one another in psalms and hymns and spiritual songs, singing with grace in your hearts to the Lord." The Word of Christ is Holy Spirit inspired Scripture that should "dwell" or "be at home" in our hearts "abundantly or extravagantly rich." Scripture should permeate every aspect of the believer's life and control every thought, word and deed. This can only take place as we are "influenced" by the Holy Spirit Who is our power and motivation. **The Holy Spirit fills the life controlled by His Word!** Sometimes I get slothful as a teacher of the Word and do not put in the study time as I should. However, when I begin to dig into the Word and my dry soul becomes a well of living water, I wonder why I waited so long.

Allowing the Holy Spirit to control my life, produces a joyful noise to the Lord and I can admonish others in psalms - good worship music; hymns - songs of praise that exalts the character and nature of God; and spiritual songs - personal songs that testify of the grace of God in my life. Over these 35 years, worship and praise has transformed my life both privately as well as publicly. That's why music is such an intricate part of my ministry and the impact it has on me, in turn, permits me to be a channel of blessing to others.

> *The greatest achievements are those that benefit others.*

Acts 16:25 says "But at midnight Paul and Silas were praying and singing hymns to God, and the prisoners were listening to them." After being beaten, their feet put into stocks and then thrown into prison, one would think that after such brutal treatment Paul and Silas would be crying "Woe is me." They indeed suffered pain and shock from the beating they had received, but at **midnight** they were praying and singing.

God sent an earthquake that shook the prison, opened the doors and loosened the chains of the prisoners. Though the jailer was about to kill himself believing that the prisoners had escaped, Paul assured him that they had not. This encounter of deliverance allowed Paul to be used to lead this jailer and his whole household to the Lord. Only a **Word filled** life could have allowed Paul and Silas to respond correctly to this bleak situation.

> *My job is to take care of the possible and trust God with the impossible.*

A "Word Filled Christian" learns to respond to life with an attitude of thankfulness. "...**in everything give thanks for this is the will of God in Christ Jesus for you.**" (I Thessalonians 5:18) This kind of attitude is not phony or put on, but an attitude that has been controlled by the Holy Spirit to give thanks not "for" everything, but "in" everything. We live in a thankless world, but God's children should always have a heart of thanksgiving because of **Whose** we are.

Growing as a "Word Filled Christian" has enabled me to be rooted and built up in Christ and established in the faith as I have been taught to abound in thanksgiving. As I yield and allow the Holy Spirit to fill me, my roots become deeper and deeper in Biblical truth. Only the Spirit establishes us in sound doctrine, but emotions will lead you into false doctrine. The Word will not always make you feel good, but it truly is good for you!

In this challenge of **Color Me A Woman of God – Break Me, Melt Me, Mold Me,** if we are not being filled or controlled by the Holy Spirit then we become like the Dead Sea, taking in but not giving out! As I continued to spiritually mature over the years,

Raymond was still unsaved. The "gulf" between us was growing wider and wider, but my love for Jesus and the Word persistently provoked me to give thanks anyway and to continue to pray for his soul.

The filling or control of the Holy Spirit enables you and I to handle the circumstances of life even as Paul and Silas. There was a time when I had to have a heart monitor because I was stressed and was not responding Biblically to situations the Lord was allowing. Other times I tried to fill the void with "buying stuff," just having any excuse to buy something new for me (it did feel good sometimes until I had to pay for it!) But the dryness was still there until I allowed the Spirit to fill my soul and give me an attitude of contentment. And guess what the Lord did? He would later allow me to get a part-time job working in a boutique where I've learned contentment. The Lord will test us in areas where we are weakest to show us how much we have grown even though He already knows.

> *Contentment isn't getting what we want but being satisfied with what we have.*

A Christlike character is a result of being filled with the Holy Spirit. We can't become like Jesus in word only, but it has to be in word and deed. My prayer truly is **"Fill me Lord until there's room for nothing more than You!!"**

Color Me a Woman of God: Fill Me!!

Color Me a Woman of God:
Use Me
(Here I Am Lord, Use Me)

God Can Do It

Longfellow could take a worthless sheet of paper, write a poem on it, and make it worth $6,000 – that's genius.

Rockefeller could sign his name to a piece of paper and make it worth a million dollars – that's capital.

Uncle Sam can take gold, stamp an eagle on it, and make it worth $20.00 – that's money.

A mechanic can take material that is worth only $5.00 and make it worth $50.00 – that's skill.

An artist can take a fifty-cent piece of canvas, paint a picture on it, and make it worth $1,000 – that's art.

ake a worthless, sinful life, wash it in the blood of
t His Spirit in it, and make it a blessing to humanity –
vation!

IN one of the cathedrals of England there is a beautiful window through which the sunlight streams. It displays the facts and personalities of the Old and New Testament and the glorious truths and doctrines of the Christian revelation. This window was fabricated by the artist out of broken bits of glass which another artist had discarded.

I, too, was once broken by the cords of sin, but God's love and forgiveness restored my fellowship with Him. God took my worthless, sinful life, washed me in His precious blood, put His Spirit in me and has given me a passion to serve Him. Just the thought of God desiring to have fellowship with me is incomprehensible! Yet, 35 years ago He began to **break me, melt me, mold me, and fill me** so that I would be equipped to be used to accomplish His purposes.

> *Expect great things from God. Attempt great things for God.*

II Timothy 2:20-21 says "But in a great house there are not only vessels of gold and silver, but also of wood and clay, some for honor and some for dishonor. Therefore if anyone cleanses himself from the latter, he will be a vessel for honor, sanctified and useful for the Master, prepared for every good work." When I think of the Church, I am not thinking of the building, but the body of Christ. In this great house, the visible church or local congregation – there are members who are vessels of honor, and vessels of dishonor, wheat and tares growing together, or the faithful and the unfaithful.

Gold and silver vessels were priceless vessels to be used on special occasions in Old Testament days. Vessels of wood and clay were vessels of dishonor...the wooden vessels used as garbage containers and the earthen vessels (pitchers and similar items) used in the performance of menial tasks. The contrast between these two vessels is not a contrast of superiority on the one hand and a humble position on the other, but of faithfulness. God calls and commissions Christians to different positions and ministries in the church, but rewards are for faithfulness in stewardship, not according to importance or position.

> *The difference between ordinary and extraordinary is that little extra.*

A usable woman is one who has matured, not numerically but experientially. Pastor Louis Greenup, Jr. says that the purpose for our life is encompassed in the fact that "our misery becomes our ministry, our pain becomes our purpose, our suffering becomes our service, our tests become our testimony, and our mess becomes our message. God allows us to hurt to heal others because we cannot heal what we cannot feel." He goes on to say, "Don't let the pain of your past punish your present and paralyze your progress and purpose." Therefore, I write this book as a testimony to God's faithfulness in the misery, pain, suffering, tests, and the mess of my life that enables His purposes to be fulfilled.

As we go through the process of being conformed to the image of Jesus Christ, we never know the means by which the Lord will encourage and instruct us. My commitment to ministry and my church always provided me with direction from the Word of God that sustained me in my walk. There was a message given by Pastor Wayne Cockrell in our Worship Service on a Mother's Day that impacted me as to the character of a woman that God uses and they all started with the letter "P." He stated that a usable woman will have (1) **A Pleasing Lifestyle;** she will be (2) **A Prepared Woman;** (3) **A Proven Woman;** and (4) **A Purposeful Woman.** My interpretations of these characteristics are the testimonies of what God has done and is doing in my life.

The first characteristic of a usable woman is that she has **A Pleasing Lifestyle.** This is witnessed in a woman whose walk has stood the test of time. **Psalms 84:11 says "For the Lord God is a sun and shield; the Lord will give grace and glory; no good thing will He withhold from those who walk uprightly."** This woman has learned over time that God is her overall provider and protector whether she is married or not. She has learned to anchor herself in Christ alone. Even when she has done more talking than walking, she will consider what she has learned and begin to let her consistent walk become proof of her talk.

My life verse **II Corinthians 5:9 "Therefore, we make it our aim, whether present or absent, to be well pleasing to Him"** again is my motivation and ambition in my Christian journey. "Aim" is from the Greek word that means "to love what is honorable." Paul demonstrated that it is right and noble for the believer to strive for excellence, spiritual goals, and all that is honorable before God. When Paul uses the term "well pleasing," it is the same as slaves who were passionate to please their masters. Even when we have sinned and grieved the heart of God and don't feel like going on because our desire is to please the Lord, this woman will accept God's forgiveness and keep running the race. The one thing that I look forward to in heaven is the fact that I won't hurt God's heart any more. I want to hear Him say **"Well done thy good and faithful servant."** So what constrains me is my love and passion for Him, even more than what I do for Him.

> *Do not follow where the path may lead - go instead where there is no path and leave a trail.*

Finding Fulfillment

Question: What are you passionate about: the things of the world, the gratification of the flesh, or intimacy with Jesus?

Challenge: Pursue Jesus in the Word, pant after Him in your heart, and press in desperation for Him in your lifestyle.

The second characteristic of a usable woman is that she is **A Prepared Woman.** How many times do we ask the Lord to use us and then when He begins to, we murmur and complain because God puts thorns on roses, while we should be praising Him for putting roses among thorns? In order to be used, we have to be **broken, melted, molded, and filled.**

A Prepared Woman is found in the story of Abigail in **I Samuel 25:2-42.** In my early Christian walk, I learned some valuable lessons from this woman that strengthened and encouraged me in my unequally yoked relationship. Abigail was married to an unsaved man named Nabal who was a wealthy rancher. His name means "fool." O.K. sisters, don't start looking up your husband's name to see what it means. During David's outlaw years, he and his followers had camped near Nabal's land and had helped protect his sheep. When sheep shearing time arrived, David sent some of his men to Nabal for appropriate remuneration, but Nabal refused their request and insulted David. When David heard this, he was furious and set out to destroy Nabal and his whole household.

> *Those who deserve love the least need it the most.*

The herdsmen shocked by David's response went to Abigail. She immediately assembled foodstuffs and set out to intercept David. Abigail's quick action and her words reveal both a special intelligence and wisdom that spared her husband and household from death. How inviting it would have been for some of us to see this kind of situation as a way out of a painful marriage and would have let David kill Nabal. But Abigail had a tender and focused heart that would not allow her to render "evil for evil." She was a strong and independent woman who had a powerful level of influence on the men in her household and she soon found out on David also.

> *Kindness is the oil that takes the friction out of life.*

God can use women who mature with wisdom and sensitivity despite their marital situations. Abigail did not allow the drunkenness of Nabal and her unequally yoked relationship to hinder her from growing in the Lord. She chose not to become bitter. Her great interpersonal skills helped her to diffuse David's anger and helped him think through the consequences of his hastily conceived intentions. She appealed to what was best in David's character as a man. What a **"Prepared Woman!"**

Abigail succeeded in turning David from his plan and so impressed him that when Nabal died of a stroke (the Lord struck Nabal) a few days later, David married Abigail. David saw her as a woman who could complement his strengths and balance his weaknesses. Like men who are secure in themselves, David found himself attracted by Abigail's obvious strengths. Only weak and insecure men are frightened of strong women. Women who have some of Abigail's qualities do themselves a disservice if they try to hide their strengths out of fear of frightening away men. (**Every Woman in the Bible, Sue and Larry Richards**)

> *The heart has no secret which our conduct does not reveal.*

Finding Fulfillment

Question: Who is the Lord using to prepare you for His glory?

Challenge: Thank the Lord now for how He is using this person's weaknesses, failures, harshness, need to control, failure to love and other sins for His purposes.

The third characteristic of a woman that God uses is that she is **A Proven Woman**. Titus 2:3 says **"…the older women likewise, that they be reverent in behavior, not slanderers, not given to much wine, teachers of good things – that they admonish the young women to love their husbands, to love their children…"** At a reception in Washington, a young man was asked by a widow to guess her age. "You must have some idea," she said, as he hesitated. "I have several ideas," he admitted with a smile. "The trouble is that I hesitate whether to make it ten years younger on account of your looks, or ten years older on account of your intelligence." What a wise young man!

The older women referred to here are those who no longer had child-rearing responsibilities, typically around age 60. I am now an "older" woman who has reached age 60 and I am so blessed to have been entrusted with these many years. I want to number my days and apply my heart to wisdom so that I can be a blessing to many more women before the Lord comes or takes me home to heaven. God is the One who has set the standard for the **Proven Woman** to be reverent in behavior.

"Reverence" can be translated "moral earnestness" and refers to moral dignity and holy behavior. We are to regard all aspects of our lives as sacred. For some time, I had compartmentalized my life – home, work, church and activities. After a few years in Christ, I finally realized that every area of my life was to be sacred – **"whatever I do in word or deed, do all in the name of the Lord Jesus..."** When I comprehended this, I understood the great accountability I have in demonstrating behavior that exemplifies Christ in every area of my life. Nothing is uglier in character than a bitter, angry, attitudinal, know it all older woman. Our reverent behavior requires:

1) that we must not be given to gossip – *Two things are bad for the heart – running up stairs and running down people.* **Proverbs 16:28 "A perverse man sows strife, and a whisperer separates the best of friends."**

2) that we not be slanderers – *Never pass up a chance to keep your mouth shut.* **Proverbs 10:18 "Whoever hides hatred has lying lips, and whoever spreads slander is a fool."**

3) that we not be given to much wine – *People know what you are by what they see, not by what they hear.* **Romans 14:21 "It is good neither to eat meat nor drink wine nor do anything by which your brother stumbles or is offended or is weak."**

4) that we be teachers of good things – *Personality has the power to open many doors, but character keeps them open.*

Proverbs 8:6 "Listen, for I will speak of excellent things, and from the opening of my lips will come right things."

The **Proven Woman's** testimony is that she has been "there" and has come through and is consistently living it out today to the glory of God. As she grows in her reverent behavior, wherever she goes she leaves a lasting fragrance. Dr. Charles Weigle composed the favorite hymn "No One Ever Cared for Me Like Jesus." One day he visited Pasadena, California. Early that morning he had an opportunity to walk through some of the famous rose gardens when the full fragrance of the flowers filled the air.

Later in the day, he arrived at the hotel where a Bible conference was being held. As he took his seat, a man turned to him and said, "Dr. Weigle, I know where you've been. You toured one of our lovely gardens, for I can smell the pleasing aroma on your clothing." Dr. Weigle replied, "My prayer is that I may walk so closely with the Lord that the fragrance of His grace will pervade my being. I want people to know by my words, actions, and songs that I have been with Jesus."

Finding Fulfillment

Question: What fragrance are you emanating – Tigress, Poison, Passion, Obsession, Beautiful, Eternity, or White Linen?

Challenge: Where it is necessary, change your fragrance either in words, actions or both.

If you have read this far, praise God for having an open and teachable spirit. Becoming transparent with lessons the Lord has taught me through these years allows me to identify with you. As the Bible states in **Titus 2:3**, the older women are to teach what is good. The reference here is to teach younger women how to function at home. Every home environment is different; therefore, you need wisdom as to how to function in your home. There is a saying, "If mama ain't happy, then no one is happy." This is a sad commentary to God's woman if the overall environment of the home is depicted by this attitude on a consistent basis.

You and I have to remember that we have a Savior Who loves us and knows the plans for our lives because **Proverbs 16:20b says ",,, and whoever trusts in the Lord, happy is he."** We are in such a crucial position to influence our husbands and children and because of this, we desperately need God's help. Therefore, I admonish you to love and pray for your unsaved or carnal husband according to God's Word. Yes, your heart is hurting, yes, you are angry and can't forgive him, yes, you want to leave, but God has not given you an open door. Christian women are walking away from their marriages as never before and abuse or infidelity is not always the factor. Instead there are personal pursuits or so called "ministry" endeavors that they think will fulfill or authenticate them instead of seeking God's purposes. The **Proven Woman** knows that God has promised not to put on her more than she can bear. She also understands that He knows when enough is enough and He can make a way of escape.

As I stated before, I did not leave and divorce Raymond because I had no scriptural grounds. I also chose not to leave because I realized that my loneliness (you don't have to be single to be lonely) and emotionally vulnerable state of mind would provide a greater avenue of attack from the enemy. Further, I didn't want to carry all of the financial weight by myself with two daughters. **Philippians 4:6 & 7 says "Be anxious for nothing, but in everything by prayer and supplication, with thanksgiving, let your requests be made known to God; and the peace of God,** which surpasses all understanding will guard your hearts and minds through Christ Jesus."

> *God always gives His best to those who leave the choice with Him.*

It's so much easier to run away from your troubled circumstances, but life without troubles is not a reality. The Bible says in **John 16:33 "These things I have spoken to you, that in Me you may have peace. In the world you will have tribulation; but be of good cheer, I have overcome the world."** As a Proven Woman, I had to understand that suffering was a part of God's curriculum. So after bringing my emotions under control and seeking the Lord's wisdom, I understood that God's grace was sufficient to keep my heart despite the holes in my umbrella. Sometimes I was not happy. It was hard adjusting to the fact that many times I had to go to special events alone. I often felt out of place sitting at Church functions with married couples and I sure couldn't identify with the singles. I also stopped counting the anniversaries in which I had planned something special and then Raymond would not go, so one day I stopped planning. He was an easy going person at times, but he was also self-sufficient. We lived in two different worlds and Jesus Christ was the dividing factor. But the Lord taught me how to have His joy as my strength in my marriage.

> *Happiness is the result of circumstances, but joy endures in spite of circumstances.*

The love that God requires here in Titus 2:3 is unconditional and is based on God's will, not on your husband's worthiness. The Greek word for love is *phileo* and emphasizes affection. The

World Book Dictionary defines affection as "a feeling of warm liking, fondness or tenderness." I learned to love Raymond unconditionally because many times I did not "like" him. Sometimes those warm feelings were just not there, so I pursued Christ to change my heart. You can't love Jesus and hate the one you live with and you sure won't pray for them if your heart is not right. Raymond's need of salvation became the motivating factor for me to love and pray for him because I did not want him to die and go to hell. If God had to come to satisfy His holiness and justice by veiling His glory in a body, suffering and dying for our sins and raising Himself from the dead, then hell must be an indescribable place of torment, and Raymond's soul became more important than my happiness.

> *There is no greater love than the love that holds on where there seems nothing left to hold onto.*

The bread-fruit tree of Australia illustrates the benefit of maturing in God's love. This tree produces fruit on its branches when it is young; on its trunk when it is middle-aged; and on its roots when it is old. My *phileo* love for Raymond took root and matured over 32 years as I yielded to the Lord and the fruit of the Spirit (love, joy, peace, longsuffering, kindness, goodness, faithfulness, gentleness, and self-control) became experiential in my life.

I not only admonish you to love your husband, but **A Proven Woman** loves her children also. Remember – you brought them into this world and they are yours. I truly thank God for my two daughters, Zena and Tasha. We had the typical growing up years as mother and daughters (me letting go, the curfews, the bumping heads), but we came through. They have blessed me with four beautiful grandchildren: Christian, Dante, Sidnee and Jayden.

Motherhood settled in my heart the fact that they were my second priority to Raymond. When Zena turned five and Tasha was born, I decided to come home from work to raise them. It was a joint decision between Raymond and I that lasted 9 years. Those were some tough times living on one income and I even remember when we raided the piggy banks until the next paycheck. However, I babysat to have spending money and never missed giving to the Lord. My house was the home that all of the kids hung out as they grew up. I would take them bowling, roller skating, the park and their favorite pastime was going to Carvel's for ice cream. When Zena and Tasha started school, we would have prayer every morning.

As they matured, financially I knew it was time for me to go back to work. My priority was to have a job which would allow me to be home when they went to and returned from school. I attended The Medix School for 6 months, received a degree as a Medical Secretary and did my internship at a hospital 5 minutes from my home. Of course, I prayed that the Lord would open a door for me to stay at this hospital so close to home.

However, when I started in May it was in a full time position. I knew school would be starting in September and I prayed that the Lord would give me the desires of my heart in regards to my children. **Psalm 37:4 says "Delight yourself also in the Lord, and He shall give you the desires of your heart."** Because there were two of us as full time secretaries in the same office, there was not enough work for both of us, so someone had to go part time. Well guess who went part time? The Lord allowed me to have the desires of my heart, hallelujah what a Savior! Throughout my daughters growing up years, the Lord provided me with working positions and hours that enabled me to keep them as a priority. My relationship with my daughters is one of love and great respect as I am their Mom, mentor and best friend.

A father, however, is the first man in a woman's life and many times her relationship with him sets the stage for how she will relate to the men who will come into her life. Zena and Tasha's relationship with their Dad was often painful because they too wanted him to know Christ. Even though Raymond was in the home, he was "not" in the home and their relationship was sometimes disconnected. They bumped heads too, but they always had respect for him. I did not have to say verbally to my daughters what they were seeing with their eyes in regards to our relationship as they matured. Yet, they too had to deal with the attitudes of their hearts and respond to their Dad with God's love. The one thing we wanted was a connected relationship with Raymond more than what he could provide for us, but he was limited in what he could give because he did not know God's love.

> *Each loving act says loud and clear, "I love you. God loves you. I care. God cares."*

It is said that a person's true character is revealed by what they do when no one is watching. Well, Zena and Tasha saw the real Cheryl behind closed doors as well as in church, and despite my failures, I thank God that I was able to **"let my light so shine before them that they could see my good works and glorify our Father in heaven."** (Matthew 5:16)

Many times people think that you are wearing a mask when they know your situation and you are not handling it the way they would. But only you and God knows what it is costing you behind closed doors, in the secret place of your heart and how you are choosing to respond. When women would find out that my husband was unsaved, they would be shocked because of the power and authority of God's Word that was demonstrated as I taught. They didn't hear vindictiveness, husband bashing, or a "woe is me" attitude. Some saints even thought that he was a "closet Christian" because of who I was, but my daughters and I knew differently. One thing I never did or any wife should do is to tear her husband down publicly. Because my husband was a very private person, I used wisdom over the years in what I would and would not share. I am only now, through the writings of this book, willing to share things that I feel will encourage other women in an unequally yoked relationship.

> *Every person should have a special cemetery lot in which to bury the faults of friends and loved ones.*

Women did not fully understand that my weakness and my hurting heart became the Lord's fertile ground for His love and Word to take root in me. Therefore, what they saw was the results of His breaking, melting, molding, and filling in order for me to be used in such a way. Even the pain of my marriage was minimized many times by the people God had placed in my life as safety nets of accountability and encouragement. As I have grown as a teacher of the Bible, my prayer is "Lord make me weak that Your strength will be made perfect."

> *I have held many things in my hands and lost them all; but the things I have placed in God's hands, those I always possess.*

Finding Fulfillment

Question: As wife and/or mother, what role or roles do you need God's specific intervention at this time?

Challenge: Seek Biblical counseling, if necessary. Find safe avenues of support and encouragement.

The fourth and final characteristic of a usable woman is that she is **A Purposeful Woman.** As I shared my testimony in the beginning of this book, the emptiness of my heart and life was the fact that I did not know why I was here on earth. In **The Purpose Driven Life** by Rick Warren, he encourages us with the answer to that question and I would recommend the reading of this book. I have indeed, however, come to know the knowledge of His will and purpose for my life as I have walked with Him these 35 years. Because He already knows the purpose for which He has made us, according to **Ephesians 3:20 "Now to Him who is able to do exceedingly abundantly above all that we ask or think, according to the power that works in us,"** He is able to complete what He has started.

When I said yes to Jesus 35 years ago, the empty place in my heart was filled by His love and I had meaning in my life. As He became at home in my heart, my foundation of faith was established and my life of service to the Lord and His people became my ministry. As my spiritual gifts developed, I had clear direction as to what would be my areas of focused ministry. As Pastor Warren says, "Purpose-driven living leads to a simpler lifestyle, a saner schedule and peace of mind." My focus was in the areas of teaching, encouragement, and ministering in music. **Ephesians 5:17 says "Therefore do not be unwise, but understand what the will of the Lord is."**

Having a focused life will have an impact on others that cross your path whether saved or unsaved. The Lord was making me a blessing to others as well as others becoming a blessing to me. He was also broadening and building relationships with other Pastors and churches around the country and other parts of the world. Understanding the Lord's will for my life to commit to an unequally yoked relationship was not easy, but it has allowed Him to do exceedingly and abundantly above all that I could ask or think.

> *In order to succeed, you must know what you are doing, like what you are doing and believe in what you are doing.*

Finding Fulfillment

Question: Do you know what God's will is for your life? If not, what is clouding your focus?

Challenge: As a wife and/or mother, your first ministry is your home, so schedule your involvement outside the home wisely. If you do know your area of giftedness, seek God's direction and opportunities to serve.

What do you do when you don't know how long things will be the way they are? **The Purposeful Woman** learns to "trust" Him!! For 32 years, I prayed for Raymond's salvation. He was the number one person on many prayer lists. But God had a "**timeline.**" On Tuesday, February 10, 2004, I had retired to bed while he was in the basement looking at television (that was his favorite pastime). At 12 midnight, he called for me to come down to the basement. When I arrived, he was having a massive stroke. He was taken to the hospital where he continued to deteriorate over the next few days.

As Raymond chose not to respond to the Gospel over the years, while hospitalized, I instructed the nurses to keep the television off. I brought in a radio, turned on a Christian station and it stayed on 24 hours a day. I wanted God's word and truth to so permeate his heart because now there was no place for him to run. By this time, he was hooked up to machines that were keeping him alive and he could only move his left hand. On Thursday, February 13, 2004, my Pastor came to see him to challenge him again regarding his salvation. After my Pastor left, I went to his bedside, took his left hand and asked him if he had asked Jesus Christ to come into his heart and, if so, to squeeze my hand. **Hallelujah!! He squeezed my hand!** I had to ask again to be sure because I had waited so long, and he squeezed it again. The word went out like lightning that after all of these years Raymond had accepted Christ.

The following Tuesday, February 17, 2004, the Lord took Raymond to heaven. **God completed in 7 days what He had been preparing for 32 years!!** Death is never something that you are prepared for no matter what kind of relationship you endured, and Raymond's death felt like a part of me had been cut away. However, on the night of his death when my daughters and I went to the hospital, we could stand around his deathbed and sing praises to our God who had been faithful to do **exceedingly and abundantly above all that we could ask or think.** On Tuesday, February 24, 2004, we had his homegoing service in which I sang praises to the glory of God. Some people asked me how could I sing and I could only tell them that God had fulfilled His Word to me and the peace of God that passed all understanding kept my heart and mind. God's purposes for my life in those 38 years of marriage were now completed.

One month later on Good Friday, six women from the Women's Prayer Ministry of my Church came to minister to me. They prepared a delicious meal that was served on the finest china and while eating, they provided comfort to me from the Word of God. After eating dinner, I was taken to my living room where I was presented with different gifts. I then was given a full body massage as Scriptures of encouragement were read to me. But the epitome of the evening was when each woman washed my foot and ministered words of blessing to me for what I had meant to them over the years. My heart was indeed overwhelmed that the Lord would ordain such a unique way of expressing His love to me.

> *Forget yourself for others and others will not forget you*

So here I am now, 4 years later, in a new season and timeframe desiring to accomplish God's will. I am a widow indeed whose home has become a haven of rest and ministry to young and older women. I have been asked many times if I would marry again and my answer to that question is "if it is the Lord's will" because I am content in the state that I am. When I was unhappy in my marriage, I wanted a David to rescue me as God provided for Abigail, but God gave no open door. I also came to realize that David had too many women. Aren't you glad when the Lord does not always give you what you want? However, as I matured and became content in my marriage, I understood that if the Lord ever provided another opportunity of marriage or healed my marriage for His glory, I wanted a "Boaz." You see this quality of man would love the Lord and His kingdom agenda first and we would become an asset and complement to each other's ministry.

Throughout those 38 years of marriage, I was blessed by the Lord to have had a wonderful and close knit family. My parents, James and Blanche Williams have celebrated 61 years of marriage and have been my greatest supporters and prayer warriors. Even now, my 86 year old father will ask me if I'm seeing anyone. Praise God, he's still looking out for his firstborn daughter! Remember my best friend Glenda of 30 years and how our relationship was always synchronized? Well the Lord closed the door for my part-time job on Thursday, May 31, 2007 and she retired on Monday, June 1, 2007. Now we both have more opportunity and privilege for full time ministry. Hallelujah!

As I seek the Lord's focused direction for my life, He has begun to open doors that I never could have imagined. Not only has He expanded my ministry of teaching and singing, but He has provided an opportunity for me to become a speaker with the ministry of Ruth Graham and Friends (the daughter of Dr. Billy Graham) on "How to be Fruitful and Fulfilled in an Unequally Yoked Relationship." The Bible says in **James 1:12 "Blessed is the man who endures temptation (trials); for when he has been approved, he will receive the crown of life which the Lord has promised to those who love Him."**

> *Success is to be measured not so much by the position that one has reached in life as by the obstacles which he has overcome while trying to succeed.*

I am now on the other side of what my Great and Awesome God purposed for my life. If I had to do it over again, I would not change anything because **He is sovereign** and nothing that I have gone through can compare to what I am now experiencing in Christ. He is indescribable, incomprehensible and truly the Altogether Lovely One and the Love of my life.

A visitor going into the studio of a great painter found on his easel some very fine gems, brilliant and sparkling. Asked why he kept them there, the painter replied: "I keep them there to tone up my eyes. When I am working in pigments, insensibly the sense of color becomes weakened. By having these pure colors before me to refresh my eyes the sense of color is brought up again just as the musician by his tuning-fork brings his string up to the concert pitch." God has made Jesus Christ the brilliant and sparkling gem of His glory and we become fruitful, fulfilled and like Him as He colors our lives by **breaking, melting, molding, and filling us in order to use us.**

> *Thank You Lord for breaking me, melting me, molding me, and filling me to use me for Your glory!!*

ABOUT THE AUTHOR

Cheryl Torain is a resident of Baltimore, Md. and is a widow with two adult daughters, Zena and Tasha, one son-in-law, Wayne, and four grandchildren: Christian, Dante, Sidnee and Jayden. She is a member of and accountable to Pastor Wayne Cockrell of the Genesis Bible Fellowship Ministries of Baltimore, Md. Cheryl currently serves as the Director of the Women's Ministry Leadership Council.

In October 1972, Cheryl Torain received Jesus Christ as her personal Savior. She teaches women at seminars, retreats, conferences, workshops, and has an extensive tape ministry. Cheryl has written a gospel tract entitled "God's Woman: His Special Creation." In August 1989, Cheryl Torain Ministries was started which encompasses her speaking and singing ministries.

Her first album, **He Cares for You, was** produced in 1989. Her sophomore effort, **From My Heart to You Lord,** was released in April 1997 on Virtue/Christ-Centered Records and was well received across the country and charted on various Gospel radio stations. On Cheryl's CD project, **Prepared to Praise** (Lifetone Records, June 2004), she served as co-producer and co-writer, having written eleven of the fifteen cuts on the disc.

Cheryl has appeared on various TV and radio stations. Cheryl's video "Have You Heard About Jesus?" was aired on **Bobby Jones BET Gospel Video**. Also, her video "Maintain" was premiered on the online television show **Virgil Taylor's Music Machine** where she had the distinct honor of being the first guest artist to be on this show.

She has had opportunities to sing and teach women in **West Africa, India and Brazil.** In 2006, she served as the Women's Ministry Leader for the Franklin Graham Festival held in Baltimore, Md. In 2008, she became one of the itinerary speakers with Ruth Graham and Friends.

The purpose for her ministry is found in **2 Corinthians 5:9 "Therefore, I make it my aim, whether present or absent to be well pleasing to Him."**

Contact Information:

Cheryl Torain Ministries
P.O. Box 66464
Baltimore, Md. 21239
Website: CherylTorain.com
Email: cat@cheryltorain.com